Corporate Acquisitions and Mergers in Peru

Corporate Acquisitions and Mergers in Peru

Third Edition

José Antonio Olaechea
María Luisa Gubbins
José Antonio Honda

Estudio Olaechea

This book was originally published as a chapter in Corporate Acquisitions and Mergers.

General Editor: Peter Begg

Wolters Kluwer

Published by:
Kluwer Law International B.V.
PO Box 316
2400 AH Alphen aan den Rijn
The Netherlands
E-mail: international-sales@wolterskluwer.com
Website: lrus.wolterskluwer.com

Sold and distributed by:
Wolters Kluwer Legal & Regulatory U.S.
7201 McKinney Circle
Frederick, MD 21704
United States of America
Email: customer.service@wolterskluwer.com

Printed on acid-free paper

ISBN 978-94-035-3353-7

e-Book: ISBN 978-94-035-3354-4
web-PDF: ISBN 978-94-035-3355-1

Printed in the United Kingdom.

Contents

Estudio Olaechea

Estudio Olaechea was founded in Lima in October 1878 and is, today, the leading and one of the largest law firms in Peru. The firm enjoys national prominence in the areas of finance, securities, privatizations and concessions, mergers and acquisitions and general international corporate work.

In order to service the specialized needs of our corporate clients and financial institutions in connection with their Peruvian activities, Estudio Olaechea has organized a Practice Group, comprised of partners and associates who are highly experienced in mergers and acquisitions. The firm has a policy of encouraging the strategy of combining legal and business skills. Our professionals have worked, studied and/or lived abroad and are familiar with international business customs and legal working schemes. Moreover, the firm has longstanding and valued professional relationships with other leading law firms around the world as well as with banks, industries, financial institutions and public sector authorities within Peru.

The firm assists companies and individuals interested in mergers and acquisitions, including due diligence and legal auditing procedures, corporate structuring, acquisition contracts, divestitures, proxy fights, joint ventures and leveraged buyouts, among other things. The firm's attorneys represent buyers, sellers, investors, shareholders' groups and financial advisers in structuring, negotiating and consummating complex domestic and international business combinations and other commercial transactions. Many of the transactions advised by the firm are international in scope.

Authors

José Antonio Olaechea, María Luisa Gubbins & José Antonio Honda

Estudio Olaechea

Bernardo Monteagudo No. 201

San Isidro

Lima – Peru

Tel.: (51–1) 219–0400

Fax: (51–1) 219–0420/(51–1) 219–0422

E-mail: Joseantonioolaechea@esola.com.pe

marialuisagubbins@esola.com.pe

Joseantoniohonda@esola.com.pe

1. LOCAL ECONOMIC, POLITICAL AND CULTURAL ASPECTS

1.1. Country Profile

[01] Peru is located in South America and is the third-largest country after Brazil and Argentina, with a land area of 1 285 216 square kilometres. It is situated in the north-west of the continent and is bordered by Ecuador and Colombia to the north, Chile to the south, Brazil and Bolivia to the east and the Pacific Ocean to the west. The coastline is 2 500 kilometres long.

[02] The country is divided into three distinct regions: the coastal region, which is a strip of land 60–100 kilometres wide; the Andes region separates the coastal desert to the west from the jungle or Amazon basin to the east and the jungle or Amazon basin, the largest region in Peru.

[03] Peru is a strategic country for countries that do not have access to the Pacific Ocean such as Brazil and Bolivia. Several highway and railroad projects are under discussion to transport merchandise from and to Brazil and to interconnect both countries with the Pacific Ocean and with the Atlantic Ocean. Peru has a strategic position for international commerce as it is located in the middle of the continent.

[04] The population of Peru is about 31 327 385. More than 70% of the population lives in urban areas and the rest in rural areas. The population growth rate is 1.2% per year. Almost one-third of the nation's population lives in Lima, the capital of Peru. Other populated and economically important cities of Peru are Arequipa, Trujillo, Piura and Cuzco.

[05] Politically, Peru is divided into twenty-four regions. The most important port of the country is located in Callao, which is very close to Lima.

[06] The principal economic activities in the coastal region are farming, agriculture, fishing, industry and tourism. In the Andes, the main economic activities are mining, tourism, agriculture and electricity. In the jungle, the main economic activities are agriculture, oil drilling, tourism and timber.

[07] Spanish is the most widely used language in the country, spoken by more than 84% of the population, followed by indigenous languages, such as Quechua and Aimara, among others.

[08] As of 31 September 2020, the exchange rate is Peruvian Sol (PEN) 3.60 per each US Dollar (USD).

1.2. Government and Political System

[09] Peru has a government that is democratic, social, independent and sovereign. The State is not divisible and its government is unitary, representative and decentralized. Some functions have been delegated to the regions in order to make the regions' decisions more efficient.

[10] The government of Peru is organized according to the principle of separation of powers.

[11] The Peruvian government is divided into three separate and independent branches: the Executive, the Legislative and the Judiciary. The Constitution defines the jurisdiction of each branch, their members and the criteria for the selection of such members.

[12] The country has been politically stable since the 1980s when the military government called for democratic elections. Since 1980, Peru has had democratic presidents elected by the popular vote of its citizens.

[13] All economic activities are open to foreign investment with no restriction on the participation of foreign investors. There are, however, some restrictions on foreign investment in certain areas of the economy, such as the media and airlines.

[14] Foreign investors have the same rights as nationals and enjoy equal legal status with these and with the State. An exception is Article 71 of the Constitution, which states that foreign investors have to obtain prior government authorization to acquire minerals, soils, water, forests, fuels or energy sources within 50 kilometres of the national border.

[15] The country is integrated into the global financial system in the 1990s after paying standing interests to 'multilateral agencies', 'bilateral creditors' and 'commercial banks', becoming fully eligible for lending and disbursement.

[16] Peru's foreign trade presence has diversified and commercial relations have been established with the Asian Pacific Economic Cooperation Association (APEC), the North American Free Trade Commerce Treaty (NAFTA), the Latin American Integration Association (ALADI), the European Union (EU), the Andean Group and Mercosur, among others. Likewise, Peru has signed free trade agreements (FTA) with several countries.

1.3. Legal System

[17] Peru has a codified civil law system.

1.4. Current Economic Aspects

[18] The year 2019 closed with an economic growth of 2.16%, adding to twenty-one years of consecutive growth. During the first quarter of 2020, the gross domestic product (GDP) registered a decrease of -3.4%, and, in the second quarter, the economy decreased considerably, at 30.2%, influenced by the worldwide pandemic COVID-19.

[19] Currently, the services sector is the most significant contributor to the country's GDP. The financial and insurance services are the main branches of this sector.

[20] As regards projections for next year, the economy should be recovered by March 2021.

[21] During 2019, less than 3% of the total transactions in the Latin American M&A market took place in Peru. This percentage refers to seventeen agreements. The investment registered pursuant to these agreements amounted to USD4 m.

[22] So far in 2019, Peru, together with Brazil, Mexico, Chile, Colombia and Argentina, led the M&A activity in Latin America. In the first quarter of 2019, Peru completed 5% of the total of M&A transactions, which refer to eleven agreements, four agreements more than the previous quarter. During the second quarter of 2019, 7% of the total transactions of the Latin American M&A market were carried out in Peruvian territory. These transactions represented an amount equivalent to USD1.665,77 m that is greater than that registered in the first quarter of 2019.

[23] Regarding the origin of the capital invested in M&A transactions in Peru in 2019, 59% of the transactions corresponded to Latin American capital, of which 47% corresponded to capital investments of Peruvian origin (eight transactions). Europe accounted for 35% of the transactions in Peru (six transactions) and Asia for 6% (one transaction). So far in 2020, the total number of transactions in Peru has decreased by 55%.

[24] Among the transactions of 2019 that can be highlighted is the acquisition by Empresa de Generación Huallaga of Investor Group (China Three Gorges Corporation).

1.5. Main Industries

[25] The Agency for the Promotion of Private Investment (PROINVERSION) reported an inflow of USD8 892 m by way of foreign direct investment in 2019. As of 31 December 2018, foreign direct investment by way of capital contributions amounted to USD5 576 m.

[26] According to PROINVERSION, as of December 2019, Spain, the United Kingdom (UK) and Chile are the three main sources of capital contributions to Peru. Together their contributions amount to 48% of the total of capital contributions.

[27] Foreign direct investment by economic sector was distributed as follows as of December 2019: Mining, Communications, Finance, Energy, Industry, Trade, Oil and Services.

[28] The main investors responsible for capital movements in the 2011–2017 period, whether through capital contributions or share purchases, were as follows: Empresa Nacional de Telecomunicaciones S.A. from Chile in Communications; Telefonica Latinoamerica Holding S.L. from Spain in Communications; Inversiones Inverfal Peru SPA from Chile in Finance; Peru Copper Syndicate LTD. from the UK in Mining; IC Power Holdings (Kallpa) Limited from Bermuda Islands in Energy; Hudbay Peru INC. from Canada in Mining; Dia Bras Exploration INC. from Canada in Finance; Ecopetrol Global Energy S.L.U. from Spain in Oil; NII Mercosur Telecom, S.L. from Spain in Communications; International Power S.A. (before Suez – Tractebel S.A.) from Belgium in Energy; Enagas Internacional S.L. from Spain in Transport and Energy; Entel Inversiones S.A. from Chile in Communications; Banco Santander S.A. from Spain in Finance; Enersis S.A. from Chile in Energy; Industrial and Commercial Bank of China Limited from China in Finance; Porcelanite Lamosa, S.A. de C.V. from Mexico in Trade; Interconexion Electrica S.A.E.S.P. from Colombia in Energy; Empresa de Energia de Bogota S.A.E.S.P. from Colombia in Energy and Oil; EEB Peru Holdings LTD. (before AEI Peru Holdings LTD.) from the Cayman Islands in Energy; Cobra Concesiones S.L. from Spain in Energy; Hidalgo e Hidalgo S.A. from Ecuador in Construction and transport; Landy S.A. from Switzerland in Finance; Britton S.A. from Switzerland in Finance.

[29] This firm's experience in the M&A world includes, among other transactions, representation of brewery SABMiller's acquisition of Bavaria's holdings in Peru (worth USD7.8 bn on a global basis); representation of SABMiller on their purchase through the Lima Stock Exchange of voting stock of Peru's largest brewery for approximately USD478 m; representation of SABMiller in six separate tender offers for the voting rights of Peru's largest brewer Union de Cervecerías Peruanas Backus y Johnston and its five listed Peruvian subsidiaries (now edging closer to 100% ownership); advisory of Maersk AS on the bid for the concession of the new terminal for containers at the Port of Callao; advisory and representation of HSBC Bank USA as security agent in the credit facility to Volcan Compañía Minera S.A.A. for USD120 m; advisory of the shareholders of Peruvian company Derivados del Maíz (DEMSA) in its sale of 100% of the outstanding common shares and 67.47% of the investment shares, and the listing of common shares on the Lima Stock Exchange; advisory of a private fund on the purchase of an important minority stake in Volcan Compañía Minera S.A.A.; advisory on the sale of Alcoa's packaging and consumer business to New Zealand's Rank group in twenty-six jurisdictions, worth 2.7 bn on a global basis; advisory of Central Parking Corporation on the sale of 100% of the shares held in its Peruvian subsidiary Central Parking System Peru S.A.; assisted all of the shareholders of Peruvian company Abrasivos S.A. in the sale of 100% of their shares in 3M Peru S.A.; advisory and representation of ACS Solutions France in various areas in regards to the concession for the Collection Unit of the Metropolitano Bus Project (Lima's main public transport service); advisory of Compañía Sudamericana de Vapores (CSAV) on its acquisition through offshore merger of a holding in Hapag-Lloyd's container business; due diligence on Maple Gas Corporation del Perú and Maple Etanol S.R.L. on behalf of Alcogroup.

1.6. Cultural Aspects

[30] Peru is a friendly place for foreign investors. Not in vain has the country achieved USD25.7 bn of foreign direct investment by way of capital contributions in the course of 2017.

[31] Good handling of the country's image has become an efficient way to promote Peru's goods and services in an increasingly competitive world market.

[32] Peru is generally regarded as a country with both an impressive geography and an impressive history. It is considered a mega-diverse country because it has 84 of the 117 existing 'life zones'.

[33] Great cultures have inhabited Peru: The Incas, Paracas, Nasca, Wari, Moche, Chimu, Tiahuanaco, among others. There are citadels like Caral, built before the Great Pyramid, where the inhabitants would gather in a circular plaza to listen to music.

[34] Peruvians are polite and always willing to assist foreigners travelling through the country.

[35] Spanish is the main language throughout Peru, although most highland Indians are bilingual, with Quechua being their preferred language and Spanish their second tongue. Several small lowland groups speak their own languages. English is understood in the best hotels, airline offices and travel agencies.

2. THE REGULATORY FRAMEWORK

2.1. Business Vehicles

[36] There are several different structures that foreign investors may use, depending on their specific needs, as investment vehicles in Peru. Peruvian Companies' Law (hereinafter, 'Corporate Law') provides for several forms of corporate organization. The most widely adopted forms are – the 'corporation' (*Sociedad Anónima*) and the 'limited liability company' (*Sociedad Comercial de Responsabilidad Limitada*). Besides these two, the Corporate Law recognizes the existence of the 'general partnership' (*Sociedad Colectiva*), the 'simple limited partnership' (*Sociedad en Comandita Simple*) and the 'limited partnership with shares' (*Sociedad en Comandita por Acciones*), among others.

2.1.1. Corporations

[37] Corporations are the most common type of business vehicle used in Peru. Their main characteristic is the limited liability of their stockholders, who are liable only to the extent of their contributions to the corporation.

[38] The capital stock is represented by shares, and there is no minimum or maximum capital requirement laid down by the law, except for certain specific types of corporations (e.g., banks, insurance companies, stockbrokers).

[39] The corporation must comprise at least two shareholders, which can be natural and/or legal entities. The duration can be for a fixed or indefinite term.

[40] The incorporation process may be carried out through simultaneous or successive subscriptions for shares. Simultaneous subscription occurs when the incorporators subscribe for all the shares themselves. Successive subscription occurs when the promoters offer the shares to the public. The shares of stock must be fully subscribed and at least 25% of each share must be effectively paid in.

[41] The board of directors and one or more managers are in charge of the administration and management of the corporation. The board of directors is composed of at least three members, and their term of office is at least one year with a three-year cap. Re-election of directors is permitted.

[42] The Corporate Law grants to the board of directors and managers certain powers to act on behalf of the corporation. However, it is conventional for the board of directors or the shareholders meeting to grant additional powers to them in connection with the performance of their duties in the corporation.

[43] The shareholders' meeting is the primary corporate body and comprises all the corporation's stockholders; they must hold a meeting at least once a year. This mandatory annual meeting must be held within the first three months of each year in order to decide the financial results of the previous year, among other issues.

[44] Different types/classes of shares may be created, including non-voting shares. Shares of stock may be freely transferred; however, restrictions on their transferability may be laid down in the by-laws (e.g., rights of first refusal).

[45] Peruvian Corporate Law distinguishes three specific types of corporations, the standard corporation, the closely held corporation and the publicly (or openly) held corporation. A corporation will be a standard corporation if it does not comply with any of the requirements established for the closely or openly held corporation.

Standard Corporation

[46] Corporations that do not comply with the requirements for publicly held or privately held corporations are considered to be standard corporations, regulated by the general clauses established for all types of corporations in the Corporate Law.

Capital Structure

[47] The corporation may issue different types or classes of shares. The difference between them could be constituted by: (1) the rights granted to their holders; (2) the obligations assumed by their shareholders; or (3) both the rights and obligations. All stocks of the same class will have the same rights and obligations.

[48] A corporation may issue non-voting stocks whether it is a standard, closely held or openly held corporation. Non-voting stocks are not counted in determining the quorum necessary to hold shareholders' general meetings. Non-voting stock confers the following rights upon the holder:

- the right to participate in the distribution of profits and net assets resulting from liquidation in priority to any common stockholder;
- the right to be informed at least every semester about the corporation's activities and management;
- the right to oppose agreements which damage their rights; and
- the right to withdraw from the corporation in cases established by the Corporate Law or the by-laws.

[49] Moreover, in the case of a capital increase, shareholders can:

- subscribe for voting stocks on a pro rata basis when the shareholders' general meeting agrees to increase the capital only through the creation of stocks with voting rights;
- subscribe on a pro rata basis for stocks with voting rights and in a sufficient number to maintain his participation in the capital, in cases where the shareholders' general meeting agrees that the increase is to include the creation of non-voting stocks (but in an insufficient number for the holders of these stocks to maintain their participation in the capital);
- subscribe on a pro rata basis for non-voting stocks in cases of capital increase where the shareholders' general meeting is not limited to the creation of stocks with voting rights or in cases where the general meeting agrees to increase the capital only through the creation of non-voting stocks; and
- subscribe for debt liabilities or other securities convertible into stocks, applying the rules set out above.

Corporate Bodies

[50] The administration and management of a corporation are carried out at the shareholders' general meetings and at the board of directors' meetings.

Corporate Bodies: Shareholders' General Meetings

[51] The shareholders' general meeting is the primary corporate body of the corporation and it comprises all of the corporation's stockholders, who must hold a meeting at least once a year. All shareholders, present, absent or dissident, are bound by the resolutions adopted at the general meeting. The meeting can be called by the board of directors, the management or by shareholders representing

20% of the subscribed shares with voting rights. The Corporate Law permits the holding of universal general meetings (without notice) when shareholders representing all the subscribed shares with voting rights are present and unanimously agree to hold the meeting.

[52] The general meeting is mandatory and must be held at least once a year within three months following the end of the corporation's fiscal year. The issues discussed include approval of the financial statements, allocation of profits, election of members to the board of directors and their compensation, designation of external auditors, and any other issue required by the by-laws or expressly stated in the call.

[53] The shareholders at the general meeting may resolve to remove the board of directors and name its successors, modify the by-laws, increase or decrease the capital, issue bonds, agree on the sale of assets whose value exceeds 50% of the corporation's capital, order investigations and special hearings, agree on the transformation, merger, spin-off, reorganization, and dissolution of the corporation, and resolve its liquidation.

Corporate Bodies: Board of Directors

[54] The board of directors is elected at the shareholders' general meeting. The by-laws will establish the minimum, maximum, or a fixed number of directors (which may not be less than three). The by-laws determine the directors' terms of office, which cannot be less than one year or more than three years. Re-election is permitted. The shareholders may remove the directors at any time without a specific cause. The position is personal unless the by-laws permit directors to be represented by others. A director is not required to be a shareholder or a resident to be elected. However, the by-laws may require this. The position may only be held by natural persons; thus, no corporation may be elected as a member of the board of directors.

[55] The Corporate Law establishes that corporations are obliged to constitute their boards of directors with appropriate representation of the minority (cumulative vote). Consequently, each share has as many votes as there are members of the board to be elected. It is possible for the minority shareholders to obtain a greater participation on the board of directors than is represented by the percentage of the share capital that they hold.

[56] The quorum for a meeting of the board of directors is 50% plus one. However, the by-laws may establish a higher quorum but may never require the attendance of all board members. Decisions are adopted by the majority of those directors attending; however, the by-laws may establish a higher requirement.

[57] It should be noted that the Corporate Law does not establish any particular requirements for the boards of directors of openly held corporations.

Closely Held Corporations

[58] The closely held corporation (*'Sociedad Anónima Cerrada'* or S.A.C.) must consist of no more than twenty shareholders. Their shares of stock cannot be registered in the Securities Market Public Registry, and thus cannot be listed on the stock exchange. The establishment of a board of directors is optional, and the shareholders have the right of first refusal to acquire the shares of any holders who wish to transfer their shares. This right of first refusal may be eliminated if it is expressly agreed to in the by-laws. Moreover, specific causes for the exclusion of stockholders can be provided for in the by-laws.

Openly Held Corporations

[59] A corporation is considered as an openly held corporation (*'Sociedad Anónima Abierta'* or S.A.A.) when the corporation meets at least one of the following requirements:

- It has more than 750 stockholders.
- It has made an initial public offering of equity or convertible debt securities.
- More than 35% of its capital stock belongs to 175 or more stockholders, without including in this number those shareholders whose personal holding of shares represents less than 0.2% of the capital or exceeds 5% of the capital.

[60] The transfer of shares of an S.A.A cannot be restricted or limited; hence, shareholders of an S.A.A do not have first refusal rights.

[61] The articles of incorporation and by-laws cannot contain clauses restricting the free transferability of shares or any type of fetter on the negotiability or marketability of the stock. They also cannot contain clauses giving a shareholder or corporation a right of first refusal to acquire shares of the S.A.A when these are transferred.

[62] The openly held corporation must have all its shares registered in the Stock Market Public Registry. The *Superintendence* of Securities Market (SMV) is the government agency in charge of supervising and controlling publicly held corporations. SMV has the following powers:

- to require the conversion of a corporation to a publicly held corporation, when appropriate;
- to demand the conversion of a publicly held corporation to another type of corporation; and
- to determine and penalize the violation of regulations laid down in the section covering openly held corporations in the Corporate Law and specific SMV regulations.

2.1.2. Limited Liability Company

[63] The limited liability company has a capital divided into participations of equal value. These are cumulative and indivisible and cannot be represented by shares of stocks. The total number of partners cannot be more than twenty. Partners are not personally liable for the company's obligations.

[64] As with corporations, there is no minimum capital requirement. However, 25% of each participation must be paid in before the incorporation can be registered at the commercial registry.

[65] Agreements within the company are achieved by the will of partners representing the majority of the capital. The by-laws can establish the manner in which these accords may be reached. However, a general meeting is mandatory when requested by partners representing at least 20% of the paid-in capital.

[66] Management of the company is performed by one or more managers, elected by the partners, and these managers may or may not also be partners. Managers are prohibited from being involved on their own behalf or on behalf of third parties in the same type of business as the company. No board of directors is required.

[67] Transferability of participations to heirs in the event of the death of a partner may be restricted by the by-laws in favour of the other partners. Partners' participations are not freely transferable to third parties. The partner must first offer his/its interests to the other partners who have pre-emptive rights to purchase them. If none of the partners exercises this right, the company may purchase such participations and amortize them, resulting in a reduction of capital. If none of this occurs, the partner in question may freely transfer his/its interests to third parties.

2.1.3. Simple Limited Partnership

[68] The simple limited partnership is a type of business organization that is formed by one or more active partners who are liable in an unlimited and joint manner for obligations incurred by the partnership and one or more non-active partners whose liability is limited to the payment of their respective contributions to the capital. These contributions cannot be represented by shares of stock or any other type of security. Unless agreed otherwise, non-active partners cannot participate in the administration of the business.

[69] To transfer contributions pertaining to active partners, the unanimous consent of the active partners and 50% plus one of the votes attributable to the non-active partners, calculated in terms of capital investment, is required. To transfer contributions of non-active partners, the agreement of 50% plus one of the votes represented by persons (active partners) and 50% plus one of the votes represented by capital (non-active partners) is required.

2.1.4. Limited Partnership with Shares

[70] The limited partnership with shares is a type of business organization that, like the simple limited partnership, has active and non-active partners with the same economic responsibilities. The difference between the two types of partnership lies in the fact that all the capital stock must be divided into shares. The active partners are in charge of the company's administration. However, non-active partners can assume responsibility for the administration, in which case such a partner would acquire the quality of an active partner.

[71] Shares belonging to active partners cannot be transferred without the consent of all of the active partners and 50% plus one of the non-active partners, calculated in terms of capital for both types of partner. Shares of non-active partners are freely transferable unless the partnership agreement establishes clauses restricting transfer.

2.1.5. Association in Participation

[72] The association in participation type of business consists of a written contractual agreement between a managing partner (*asociante*) and a contributing partner (*asociado*). This agreement can be executed by two or more natural persons or legal entities for the purpose of executing a particular business or project. The agreement is not subject to registration with the commercial registry.

[73] The managing partner of an association in participation agrees to grant the contributing partner a participation in the results or profits of one or more businesses of the managing partner in exchange for a fixed contribution such as money, property, or services, to the enterprise or project. The managing partner acts in his own name and the association in participation has no legal name. Management of the business enterprise is solely performed by the managing partner who is the only person responsible to third parties.

[74] Unless stated otherwise in the agreement between the parties, the contributing partner participates in the losses in the same percentage as he participates in the profits. In any event, losses cannot exceed the amount of the contributing partner's contribution.

[75] The managing partner cannot include third parties in the business without the written consent of the contributing partner.

[76] The assets contributed by the contributing partner are presumed to belong to the managing partner unless these assets are recorded in the commercial registry under the name of the contributing partner.

[77] These types of agreement undeniably offer a number of advantages and are an excellent mechanism to satisfy the interests of the parties in initiating new business endeavours, extending and optimizing existing ones and accessing new markets.

[78] The association in participation is an associative structure that has similar purposes to those of a corporation, but should not be confused with it. The essential differences between them are:

- The agreements are not revealed to third parties because they are private contracts between the parties.
- They are not subject to publicity formalities.

- The agreements do not give rise to the formation of a legal entity as corporations do.
- The economic collaboration does not imply the formation of a common capital fund.
- There is no common commercial name; the business continues to belong to the managing partner.

2.1.6. Consortium

[79] A consortium is an agreement by which two or more persons actively and directly participate in a specific project or enterprise to obtain economic benefits. Each party maintains its own autonomy. Each member performs the activities entrusted to them by the consortium or assumed by them. When doing so, each party must coordinate his activities with the other members of the consortium according to the procedures and mechanisms established in the agreement.

[80] The assets contributed to the consortium remain the property of the relevant member contributor. Any joint acquisition of assets is governed by the rules of the joint ownership regime.

[81] Each member of the consortium is individually responsible to third parties for his/its activities within the consortium. Any liabilities and responsibilities involved are assumed at the member's own risk.

[82] If the consortium enters into an agreement with third parties, the responsibility is shared among the consortium members, unless stated otherwise in the agreement or by law.

[83] The consortium agreement must establish the relative participation of each member in the profits and losses. Otherwise, participation will be understood to be on an equal basis for each member.

2.2. Main Compliance, Registration and Reporting Requirements of the Most Common Forms of Business Vehicle

[84]

- All Peruvian companies are required to file monthly and annual tax returns with the tax authority. In addition, all transfers of shares and changes of legal representatives must be notified to such authority.
- All Peruvian companies are required to register with the Peruvian Public Registry certain resolutions adopted by the shareholders meeting or by the board of directors meeting, including among others any capital increases, mergers, acquisitions, dissolution, or any other changes to the by-laws.

3. LAWS AFFECTING MERGERS AND ACQUISITIONS

[85] The main laws and regulations affecting M&A transactions in Peru are the following:

(a) Law No. 26887 – Peruvian Companies' Law.
(b) Peruvian Civil Code, approved by Legislative Decree No. 295.
(c) Peruvian Tax Code, approved by Supreme Decree No. 33-2013-EF.
(d) Peruvian Income Tax Law, approved by Supreme Decree No. 179-2004-EF.
(e) Securities Market Law, Legislative Decree No. 861, amended by Law No. 27649.
(f) CONASEV Resolution 009-2006-EF/94.10.
(g) Pre-M&A merger control regulations, approved by Supreme Decree No. 013-2019.

[86] Pre-M&A merger control regulations have been created to guarantee free competition in the internal market.

[87] Also note that, while it is not directly a merger control regulation, the transfer of 10% or more of the capital stock of a banking, financial or insurance company to a sole person requires prior authorization from the Superintendency of Banking, Insurance and Pension Funds (SBS). This rule applies even if such transfer is made indirectly through third parties.

[88] Authorization from the SBS will also be required if a sole person reaches the percentage referred to above in stages by a number of transactions.

[89] In such cases the SBS will evaluate the financial and moral solvency of the buyer and will verify that there are no applicable constraints on the buyer holding the said percentage of a financial or insurance company. The SBS does not evaluate the transaction itself.

3.1. Acquisition of Companies Listed on the Stock Exchange

[90] The acquisition of companies listed on the Stock Exchange and registered with the SMV is subject to specific rules laid down in the Securities Market Law, Legislative Decree No. 861, amended by Law No. 27649.

3.2. Takeover Bids for a Significant Stake (OPA)

[91] Article 68 of the Securities Market Law regulates takeover bids for a significant stake. Article 68 states as follows:

> Individuals or legal entities intending to acquire or increase directly or indirectly, in a single transaction or in several transactions, a significant stake in a company that has at least one class of stocks with voting rights listed on an exchange, shall make a tender offer addressed to the holders of stocks with voting rights and of other securities which may confer voting right in such company.

[92] The scope of these concepts of 'a significant stake' and of 'an increase in a significant stake' was first defined in CONASEV Resolution 630-1997-EF/94.10, which regulated the conduct of tender offers. Later, CONASEV Resolution 009-2006-EF/94.10 came into force on 3 May 2006 and amended this concept. It established that a significant stake consists of any direct or indirect ownership of stocks with voting rights representing 25% or more of the capital of a company which has at least one type/class of stock with voting rights registered on a stock exchange. Likewise, a significant stake will be regarded as obtaining in any situation where a person or a group of persons, without having direct or indirect ownership, exercises voting rights over stocks with voting rights representing a percentage equal to or greater than 25% of the capital stock of a company, or where the acquirer has sufficient shares or voting rights: (i) to remove or appoint a majority of the directors; or (ii) to amend the by-laws.

[93] Article 4 of this CONASEV Resolution states that there is an obligation to make a tender offer (OPA) when the following occurs:

(i) the transfer is onerous;
(ii) the company subject to the OPA has at least one class of stocks with voting rights, or capable of conferring voting rights;
(iii) the transfer may result in the acquirer reaching or exceeding an interest of 25%, 50% or 60% (as the case may be) in the capital stock of a company, subject to the OPA, or that the acquisition is made for shares which (whether by contract or voting rights or otherwise) carry the right to remove or appoint a majority of the directors or to amend the by-laws; and
(iv) none of the exceptions set out in Article 10 of CONASEV Resolution No. 009-2006-EF/94.10 are met (e.g., the acquisition of American Depositary Receipts (ADRs), Global Depositary Receipts (GDRs) or similar securities unless the holder exercises the voting rights attributable to the underlying shares or requests the delivery of the said shares or exercises first refusal rights, among other cases).

[94] The OPA must be addressed to all the holders of stocks with voting rights, or of securities capable of conferring voting rights, of the issuer. CONASEV Resolution No. 009-2006-EF/94.10 has established that the purpose of the OPA is to guarantee that when an acquisition of a significant stake (or the increase of a significant stake) occurs, all the shareholders can participate in the control premium that may be offered.

[95] Finally, an OPA is not mandatory when the total number of stockholders with voting rights of the issuer unanimously agree to sell or exchange all or part of their stocks with voting rights.

[96] In circumstances where a significant stake is acquired without an OPA in: (i) a single transaction; or (ii) in no more than four separate transactions within a period of three years, it will be mandatory to make a 'Subsequent OPA' after the acquisition, which will have to be directed to the remaining shareholders in order to allow them to sell part of their shares. The percentage of their shares which will be subject to the 'Subsequent OPA' is determined according to the following formula:

$$[X/Y] \times [1-Z]$$

Where:

X = the percentage of shares acquired in the last three years or in a single transaction.

Y = the percentage held by third parties before the acquisition or series of acquisitions that reach the significant stake limit.

Z = the percentage of shares held by the acquiring party after the acquisition transaction or series of transactions within the last three years that reach the significant stake limit.

3.3. Tender Offer by Exclusion from the Registry

[97] Article 69 of the Securities Market Law, Legislative Decree No. 861, amended by Law No. 27649, regulates offers to purchase listed securities as a result of their exclusion from the Registry. Article 69 of this amended rule states as follows:

> The exclusion of a security from the Registry determines the joint and several liability of those who were responsible for it, to make an offer to purchase the securities to be delisted to the remaining holders of those securities. The offer price shall not be less than the quotation set in accordance with the criteria set forth by the SMV by means of a rule of general character. If such quote is not available, the minimum price shall be determined by an auditing firm, bank, investment bank or consulting company designated by the SMV, for account of those responsible for the delisting, in accordance with internationally accepted valuation practices. The price shall be stated and paid in cash, within the deadline established for the settlement of cash transactions. In case of securities registered or negotiated in centralized mechanisms, the tender offer shall be made in those centralized mechanisms.

[98] Thus, the purpose of the purchase offer by exclusion from the Registry (delisting) is to establish a mechanism for *the* benefit of those investors who are not agreeing with or not participating in the decision to exclude/delist the registered security, who may consider themselves to be affected by the said exclusion/delisting.

[99] It is not *mandatory* to carry out a purchase offer by exclusion from the Registry in cases of mergers or spin-offs, when the securities of the absorbing company or the securities resulting from the merger, or the spin-off company and its beneficiaries, if applicable, are registered in the Registry.

3.4. Disclosure of Interests: Listed Shares

[100] Resolution No. 005-2014-SMV-01 dated 17 March 2014 and in force since 1 July 2014 established rules for the disclosure of important facts relating to issuers of primary and secondary public offers of securities. Important facts include, for this purpose, mergers and spin-offs of the issuer as well as the issue of shares, debentures or other debt securities to be placed in Peru and/or abroad by private or public offer.

[101] In the case of a merger, the issuer is obliged to file the following information with the SMV:

(i) a copy of the approved merger agreement project;
(ii) the date on which the merger agreement project will be in force;
(iii) the financial statements and any other economic and financial information which formed the basis for the adoption of the merger agreement of the companies involved;
(iv) general and particular criteria, duly supported, to be used in the valuation of assets, the liabilities of each of the companies involved in the merger, and the method of application;
(v) the relationship between the paid-up capital and investment shares before the merger;
(vi) if applicable, the benefits agreed to be distributed to the holders of capital stock or investment stocks, as well as any other particular privileges;
(vii) the basis of the share exchange ratio, including charts with the respective supporting material and the method of calculation;
(viii) the issuer must give notice of its intention to maintain the listing of the shares in the stock market or of its intention to delist them, if applicable.

[102] Within fifteen working days of registration of the merger in the public registry, the issuer or, if applicable, the absorbing or incorporated company must deliver the final balance sheet and the public deed of merger to the SMV.

[103] Additionally, an important fact that must be notified to the SMV is the transfer of shares representing 10% or more of the subscribed and paid-up capital, as soon as the transfer has been notified to the issuer. By way of confidential information, the issuer must communicate to the SMV the start of any negotiations intended to result in the potential acquisition of a quantity of securities which would oblige the issuer to formulate a public tender offer.

[104] Important facts must be notified to the SMV on the working day on which the agreement has been adopted or the fact has happened.

3.5. Unlisted Shares

[105] According to the General Companies' Law, there is no obligation to disclose share interests in unlisted companies.

[106] A mandatory tender offer of listed securities with voting rights must take place:

> *Upon the acquisition or increase of a significant stake when: (i) it has been made indirectly, (ii) as a result of a public offering, (iii) by the following procedures:*
>
> – when the significant stake is transferred to the purchaser in a single act; or
>
> – if the significant stake is acquired through no more than four successive acts within a period of three years.

[107] Another kind of non-mandatory bid is one made prior to the acquisition or the increase of a significant stake in all *other* cases. In these cases, the bid must be made for the number of listed securities with voting rights to be acquired.

[108] The buyer cannot make a partial offer. The buyer can improve the offer, even if there has not been another offer. This improvement, however, can only be effected within the deadline set for the submission of competing offers.

[109] There is a duty to report all purchases of securities and shares of listed companies to the SMV.

[110] The target company must issue a report to its shareholders, informing them of the advantages and disadvantages of accepting the tender offer. The financial statements of a listed company must be disclosed and published on the website of the SMV where anyone can have access to it.

3.6. Announcements

[111] A notice must be issued by the relevant stock exchange in their daily newsletter throughout the procedure of the tender offer. In addition, such notice must be published by the bidder, for once, in the Official Gazette *El Peruano* and in another newspaper having the widest circulation of the domicile of the target company, within two days following the initiation of the tender offer.

[112] In this context, the SMV and the bidder must make available free copies of the prospectus to interested parties.

[113] The minimum price to be offered in the public bid:

(a) The value arising from the contribution or weighted average price during the three months immediately preceding the filing of the application or the occurrence of any of the events provided for in Article 31 of CONASEV Resolution 009-2006-EF/94.10.

(b) The value determined by a valuation company. This valuation is subject to the provisions of Title IV of CONASEV Resolution 009-2006-EF/94.10.
(c) The consideration offered in the tender offer must be qualitatively and quantitatively the same for all recipients of the offer and may consist of cash, securities or a combination of both.
(d) The securities offered as consideration must first be registered in the capital market registry.

4. RELEVANT REGULATORY AUTHORITIES

[114] The main governmental and regulatory authorities regarding the securities market and banking regulation are the following.

4.1. Securities Market Regulator

[115] The SMV is a specialized technical entity that regulates the capital market in Peru. The SMV is an entity under the Ministry of Economy and Finance and aims to ensure the protection of investors, the efficiency and transparency of the markets under its supervision, and the orderly pricing and dissemination of all information necessary for such purposes. The SMV is a legal entity of internal public law and enjoys functional, administrative, economic, technical and budgetary autonomy.

[116] The functions of the SMV are, among others, the following:

(a) To enact rules to regulate the capital market, the market for financial products and the collective funds system and to supervise corporate law compliance.
(b) To monitor compliance with the laws of the capital market, the financial products market and the collective funds systems, by natural and legal persons involved in those markets.
    Natural or legal persons subject to the supervision of the SBS are also under the supervision of the SMV on issues involving participation in the capital market under the supervision of the SMV.
(c) To promote and study the capital market, the financial products market and the pension funds system.

[117] It also falls to the SMV to monitor compliance with international auditing standards by audit firms authorized by an accountants association in Peru and hired by natural or legal persons subject to the supervision of the SMV in compliance with the norms under its jurisdiction, to which it may impart general provisions consistent with international auditing standards and from whom it may require any information or documentation to verify such compliance.

4.2. Superintendence of Banking, Insurance and Pension Funds

[118] SBS is a constitutional independent organ intended to protect the interests of the public, cautioning stability, solvency and transparency of natural or legal persons under its supervision, to promote greater financial inclusion and to contribute to the system of prevention and detection of money laundering and terrorist financing.

[119] The functions of SBS include, among others, the following:

(a) Authorizing the organization and operation of legal entities carrying out any of the operations specified in the General Law of the Financial and Insurance Systems and Organic Law of the Superintendence of Banking, Insurance and Pension Funds.
(b) Ensuring compliance with laws, regulations, statutes, and all other provisions governing the 'financial system' and the 'insurance and private pension funds management system', by exercising complete control over any and all operations, business and generally any legal act conducted by the supervised companies.
(c) Exercising overall supervision of financial, insurance and private pension funds companies, as well as those incorporated by special law that are under its supervision.
(d) Supervising natural or legal persons placing funds in Peru.
(e) Interpreting, in accordance with the administrative provisions of the ordinary law and the general principles of law, the scope of laws governing the financial, insurance and private pension funds companies, as well as those carrying out additional services, being its decisions binding administrative precedents.
(f) Enacting the necessary regulations to conduct financial and insurance operations in an appropriate manner.
(g) Issuing necessary regulation to ensure that supervised entities comply adequately with agreements signed by the Republic of Peru to combat money laundering and/or terrorist financing.
(h) Providing risk identification with respect to each supervised company separately.
(i) Issuing regulations to clarify the preparation, presentation and publication of financial statements, and any other complementary information, verifying that such statements reflect the actual financial situation of the supervised companies, as well as the rules for the consolidation of financial statements in accordance with generally accepted accounting principles.
(j) Entering into cooperation agreements with other supervisory and related entities in other countries, in order to improve the overall level of supervision.
(k) Implementing and enforcing the regulations and supplementary provisions about money laundering and/or terrorist financing.

4.3. Timing Matters

[120] All of the regulatory bodies referred to above have an exclusive administrative document of established procedures, detailing their deadlines and indicating the range of time that each such body can take to solve or answer any paperwork or procedure.

[121] Each deadline or range of time depends on the relevant procedure to be used. It cannot be used/abused to expedite or accelerate the issue of permits.

5. CONTROLS/RESTRICTIONS ON FOREIGN INVESTMENT

[122] Foreign investment in Peru is unrestricted, save for: (i) the prohibition contained in Article 71 of the Peruvian Political Constitution which states that foreign investors are not allowed to acquire minerals, soils, water, forests, fuel and energy sources within 50 kilometres of the national border; and (ii) certain economic activities for which specific authorization to invest is required.

[123] In spite of this, foreign investors generally speaking enjoy the same rights as nationals and enjoy equal legal status with the State.

5.1. Regulated Areas

5.1.1. Defence

[124] Article 44 of the Peruvian Political Constitution establishes that the State has a primary role, among others, in the security or defence of the country. Hence, Article 175 establishes that only the Armed Forces and the National Police can use and/or own war weapons. Any existing, manufactured weapon of this type coming into the country will automatically be owned by the State without any compensation procedure.

[125] The manufacture of other weapons by private industry is regulated by the Manufacture, Use and Possession of Weapons by Private Individuals Act. A legal entity establishing a business for the manufacture of weapons and ammunition for private use requires an authorization issued by the National Superintendence of Control of Security Services, Weapons, Ammunition and Explosives for Civil Use (SUCAMEC). A foreign company wishing to manufacture and sell weapons and ammunition for private use must request the relevant authorization from SUCAMEC.

5.1.2. Banking and Insurance

[126] The General Law of the Superintendence of Banking, Insurance and Pension Funds ensure equal treatment of all investments, whether by nationals or foreigners, which means the same rights and obligations for all in relation thereto.

[127] Nevertheless, all non-Peruvian entities within the financial and insurance system aiming to establish a branch or agency in Peru must have prior authorization from the Banking and Insurance Superintendence.

[128] The period required for obtaining such an authorization is approximately 220 calendar days for the establishment authorization and 120 calendar days for the operating authorization.

5.1.3. Pension Fund Management

[129] According to the Private System of Pension Fund Management Act, which governs the terms of the tendering procedure for a Pension Fund Manager (AFP), a non-Peruvian legal entity could apply for a tendering procedure but must have a prior certificate and/or authorization to create an AFP issued by the Superintendence of Banking, Insurance and Pension Funds. Such an authorization takes approximately ninety-one business days for the establishment authorization and sixty business days for the operating authorization.

5.1.4. Broadcasting

[130] According to the Peruvian Radio and Television Act, only natural persons of Peruvian nationality or legal entities incorporated and domiciled in Peru are allowed to be authorized and to be licence holders. A non-Peruvian cannot be a licence or authorization holder, either directly or indirectly through a corporate entity owned by such a person.

[131] An application for a broadcasting authorization must be submitted to the Ministry of Transport and Communications. The Ministry will take into account the principle of reciprocity and the legislation regulating foreign ownership of broadcasting companies in the country of origin.

5.1.5. Energy

[132] The Decree-Law of Electrical Concessions allows natural or legal persons, whether Peruvian or not, to control the generation, transmission and distribution of electric power.

5.1.6. Aeronautical Transportation

[133] Commercial transportation within the country itself (national) is reserved to Peruvian legal entities. No foreigners are allowed to obtain an operating permit for national transportation. To be considered a Peruvian legal entity, the company in question must:

(a) duly be incorporated under Peruvian law, have its domicile in Peru and have as its corporate purpose the undertaking of commercial aviation. To be considered as domiciled, it must carry on its main activities and install its head office administration in Peru;
(b) have more than one-half of the directors, managers and/or individuals who control the company's management as Peruvians domiciled in Peru or, in the case of foreigners, they must either be domiciled or habitually resident in Peru in order to qualify towards this percentage; and
(c) have at least 51% of the company's capital stock must be owned by Peruvians and the company must be under the genuine and effective control of shareholders and partners domiciled or habitually resident in Peru. Six months after obtaining the operating permit, this percentage could be reduced to 30% of Peruvian origin.

International aviation is not subject to any such restrictions.

5.1.7. Maritime

[134] Law No. 28583, Law on Reactivation and Promotion of the National Merchant Marine states that all commercial maritime activities are reserved exclusively for those bodies qualifying as a National Shipping Company (NSC).

[135] To qualify as an NSC, the following requirements must be fulfilled:

(i) If it is a legal entity it must:
  (a) be incorporated in Peru;
  (b) have its main domicile in Peru;
  (c) have a total of 51% of its subscribed and paid-up capital owned by Peruvian citizens. This requirement is fulfilled if the ultimate indirect ownership is held by Peruvian citizens;
  (d) have its chairman, the majority of its directors as well as its general manager as Peruvian citizens domiciled in Peru.
(ii) It must be engaged in aquatic transportation services either for domestic (cabotage) and/or for international traffic.
(iii) It must own a Peruvian flag vessel or be a lessee of such a vessel in the form of a leasing or a bareboat charter, with the option of mandatory purchase.
(iv) It must have an Operation Permit (OP) from the General Directorate of Authorizations in Transport of the Ministry of Transport and Communications (DTA).
(v) It must show that it has a minimum capital representing 5% or more of the estimated value of the vessel to be purchased. As soon as a vessel is acquired, the capital must be adjusted to an amount equal to 15% of the vessel's value owned by the NSC.

[136] The OP is the official authorization issued by the DTA for an indefinite term for carrying on maritime, river and lake transportation activities.

[137] Prior to the granting of the OP, the DTA could issue a temporary OP, valid and providing the relevant benefits for 180 labour days, allowing for the acquisition of the vessel or the leasing or the bareboat charter with the option of mandatory purchase.

[138] The term of the temporary OP will become indefinite after the NSC acquires a vessel and files with the DTA all the requirements for its qualification as an NSC in accordance with the regulation.

[139] On 7 August 2019, Legislative Decree No. 1413 which promotes and facilitates Maritime Transport in Passenger and Cargo Cabotage Traffic took effect since its Regulations have been issued and approved by Supreme Decree No. 029-2019-MTC. The requirements to perform maritime cabotage traffic of passengers and cargo are the following:

(i) To be incorporated in Peru with share capital of national or foreign origin.
(ii) To have an Operating Permit (OP).
(iii) To have a Certificate of Transportation Security Conditions (CTSC).

Compliance with requirements (i) and (ii) is excepted for three years. The authority will evaluate its impact and decide whether or not to continue the exception after that period.

5.2. Participation in Business Organizations

[140] As foreign investors have the same rights as nationals, there is generally no problem for a foreign purchaser to acquire a 100% interest.

[141] However, as referred to above, there are certain activities that require a major participation of national investors. In this respect, those activities include:

(i) *Aeronautical:* The Civil Aviation Act states that for national commercial aviation at least 51% of the capital stock must be owned by, and be under the real and effective control of a Peruvian shareholder or partner with permanent domicile in Peru. For a period of six months from the effective date of the operating permit, there cannot be majority control by foreigners. When this period ends, the percentage of capital stock owned by foreigners may be up to 70%.

(ii) *Maritime*: Law No. 28583, Law on Reactivation and Promotion of the National Merchant Marine states that to qualify as a National Ship Owner or an NSC the ownership of the corporation must be national and at least 51% of the paid-up capital stock of the corporation must be subscribed and owned by Peruvian citizens. These requirements continue to apply to the marine transport of bulk liquids other than liquefied natural gas. The maritime transport of passengers and cargo on the Peruvian coast are not included within this restriction and are governed by Legislative Decree No. 1413.

5.3. Foreign Ownership Restrictions

[142] The only absolute restriction on foreign ownership is that stated in Article 71 of the Peruvian Political Constitution mentioned in paragraph **[122]**.

[143] The rules referred to above cannot be circumvented by acquisition through a locally formed Special Purpose Vehicle (SPV) owned by foreign interests because the Peruvian Political Constitution and Acts referred to above state the absolute restriction and the requisite domestic/national percentages for corporations wishing to undertake such activities.

5.4. Restrictions on Corporate Bodies

[144] For the following activities, there are special requirements. The restrictions are as follows:

(i) *Aeronautical*: The Civil Aviation Act states that at least a half plus one of the directors, managers and people responsible for the control and direction of the corporation should be of Peruvian nationality or have a permanent domicile in Peru.

(ii) *Maritime*: Law No. 28583, Law on Reactivation and Promotion of the National Merchant Marine states that the chairman of the board of directors, a majority of the directors and the general manager must be of Peruvian nationality and domiciled in Peru.

[145] The presence of a governmental official is not required on the administrative structure of the corporation.

5.5. Permissions to Trade

[146] Permits to trade are not generally required. However, whether for foreign or national investors, trading in certain products (such as controlled chemical products) needs the permission or authorization of relevant competent authorities.

5.6. Minimum Capital Requirements and Restrictions

[147] There are no minimum capital requirements for foreign-owned companies.

[148] The only restriction on a foreigner or foreign-owned company owning land, mining/mineral rights or other immovable property is that stated in Article 71 of the Constitution mentioned in paragraph **[122]**.

6. INCENTIVES FOR FOREIGN INVESTMENT

6.1. Investment Incentives

[149] Peruvian regulation has established several tax incentives for foreign investors, such as:

- Value Added Tax (VAT) Special Advance Recovery Regime applicable for any kind of individual or legal entity who carry out investments in any financial sector generating 'third-category' income and who are in the pre-production stage of the project for which the benefit is requested.
- Promotion of regional and local public investment involving the participation of the private sector. This law established an incentive for investors in general (whether Peruvians or foreigners).
- Special tax regime for the promotion of the Agricultural Sector in order to promote agro-industrial investment. This regime has special benefits from income tax and also VAT for certain activities (e.g., crops and/or livestock activities). These tax benefits are in force until 31 December 2021.
- Tax regime for promoting regional and local investment as free taxes zones (e.g., special development zones and free zones). There are exemptions from income tax and local taxes.
- Promotion of Investment for the Peruvian Amazon Region. Tax benefits as a lower tax rate from income tax and exemption from VAT will be in force until 31 December 2029.
- Incentives to promote real estate investment funds through Real Estate Investment Funds (FIRBI) and Real Estate Investment Securitization Trusts (FIBRA).
- Special Deduction of Expenses Regime for projects of scientific research, technological development and innovation.
- Tax Stability Agreements.
- FTA.

6.2. Special Tax Exemptions

[150] The Income Tax Law establishes a number of exemptions for certain persons and operations, including, among others: (i) an exemption for interests arising from credits or financing granted by international organs or governmental foreign institutions; (ii) an exemption for royalties obtained from advisory work in technical, economic, financial or similar matters rendered externally by international entities or governmental organizations; and (iii) an exemption for interests or any profits arising from external credits granted to the Peruvian Public Sector. Additionally, a temporary exemption on income tax until 31 December 2019 has been approved through Law No. 30341 for incomes derived from the transfer of shares carried out through the Lima Stock Exchange provided certain requirements are met.

[151] The Income Tax Law also establishes an exemption for companies providing international transportation services between Peru and foreign countries, provided that an exemption is granted to Peruvian lines on a reciprocal basis in those foreign countries.

6.3. Economic Zones

[152] *Special Development Zones* (ZED) currently operating are located in Ilo, Matarani and Paita. ZED Tumbes, Loreto and Puno are created by law but these have not been implemented so far. Any company which is established in these zones is exempted from income tax, VAT and any kind of taxes, contributions or payments to the Public Treasury related to taxes, rates or contributions. Exemptions are in force until 22 May 2048 in the case of Loreto and until 31 December 2042 in the case of Ilo, Matarani and Paita.

[153] Free Zone of Tacna – ZOFRATACNA is an area where activities such as industrial, agro-industrial, distribution, unpacking, maquila and services may be carried on. Any kind of user located in ZOFRATACNA that carries out such activities will be exempted (for those operations and activities only) from income tax, VAT and any kind of taxes, contributions or payments to the Public Treasury related to taxes, rates or contributions.

[154] On the other hand, the users of ZOFRATACNA may enter machinery, equipment, tools, spare parts and construction materials of foreign origin, for the development of their activities, enjoying a special regime of suspension of the payment of customs duties and other taxes levied on the importation. The merchandise entered into ZOFRATACNA may remain stored until 2042.

[155] Special Economic Zone of Puno – ZEEPUNO has similar exemptions as ZOFRATACNA. However, it is not operating yet.

6.4. Legal Stability Agreements for Private Investments

[156] Legislative Decree No. 662 establishes and guarantees the legal stability of certain agreements for foreign investment – i.e., certain legal provisions in force at the time the investment was made will remain in force. Legal provisions that can be frozen in this way include tax laws, free access to foreign exchange and the right to non-discriminatory treatment as between investors in companies on the basis of national or foreign participation. This legal stability is granted for ten years.

[157] Foreign investors do not need any type of authorization to repatriate/transfer abroad funds from capital, profits, dividends and royalties. These funds can be transferred in freely convertible currency after taxes have been paid.

[158] Investments in foreign currency do not need any prior official authorization. There is complete freedom to hold and dispose of foreign currency in Peru, and its value is set by market supply and demand. The exchange rate is based on a floating rate.

[159] Moreover, there are no restrictions on the flow of capital. Investors are allowed to use foreign currency to purchase foreign goods and to cover their financial obligations. Individuals and companies may maintain bank accounts in foreign currencies, either in local or in foreign banks.

6.5. Guarantees in Respect of Foreign Investment

[160] Investors are authorized to contract insurance within Peru and abroad, in order to protect their investments from commercial and non-commercial risks. The government offers investors' coverage to protect their investments through the World Bank's Multilateral Investment Guarantee Agency (MIGA) – an agreement ratified by the Peruvian Congress on 2 April 1991.

[161] Moreover, Peru has signed the Covenant with the United States' (US) Overseas Private Investment Corporation (OPIC), ratified by the Peruvian Congress on 14 May 1993.

[162] Likewise, Peru has signed bilateral investment agreements with countries such as the US, Korea, Switzerland, Thailand, Bolivia, Great Britain, France, Paraguay, Singapore, the Czech Republic, Colombia, Canada, Sweden, Italy, Romania, Chile, Cuba, Ecuador, China, Japan, Argentina, Spain, Portugal, Denmark, the Netherlands, Germany, Norway, Finland, Malaysia, El Salvador, Australia, Venezuela, Mexico, Costa Rica, Panama, the European Association of Free Commerce, the Economic Cooperation Forum Asia-Pacific, Member States of MERCOSUR (Argentina, Brazil, Paraguay and Uruguay) and the Economic Union formed by Belgium and Luxembourg. Peru has subscribed the Comprehensive and Progressive Agreement for Trans-Pacific Partnership, with ratification pending, and it will come into force once ratified by at least 50% of the signatories. Also, Peru will have future negotiations with Russia, Morocco, India and South Africa.

[163] Peru has signed conventions for avoiding double taxation with Canada, Chile, Brazil, Mexico, Switzerland, Portugal, the Republic of Korea and the member countries of the Andean Community (Colombia, Ecuador and Bolivia).

6.5.1. Financing

[164] Most Peruvian financing is obtained from banks, finance companies, branches of foreign banks, leasing companies, factoring companies, trustee services companies, investment banks, municipal savings and loan banks, and even from bank syndicates.

6.5.2. Financing Mechanisms

[165] The Banks may carry out all types of financial transactions, including the acquisition of securities, the purchase and sale of gold and precious metals, leasing operations, acting as trustees where trusts involve investment management, the issue of bonds and debentures, financial advisory services, management of mutual funds (only through a subsidiary), brokerage activities, underwriting and warehousing (only through a subsidiary).

[166] Finance companies are institutions obtaining public resources which specialize in facilitating the placement of primary securities' issues, operating with bearer securities and rendering advisory services of a financial nature.

[167] Foreign banks can establish branches in Peru after complying with the requirements established by the SBS. The foreign branch will enjoy the same benefits and be subject to the same obligations as any Peruvian financial company.

[168] Leasing companies are institutions specializing in the acquisition of personal property and/or real estate to be assigned for the use of a natural or legal person in return for the payment of a periodic rent, and with the option to buy such property for a predetermined value.

[169] Factoring companies are institutions which specialize in the acquisition of invoices approved by the payer, securities and generally any commercial paper which represents debt.

[170] Trustee companies specialize in acting as trustees in the management of autonomous trustee equity, or in the carrying out of trusteeships of any nature. Trusteeship is a legal relationship whereby the trustor transfers property under trust to another person, the fiduciary or trustee, for the setting up of a trust in respect of that property, subject to compliance with a specific end in favour of a trustor or a third party. Such trust property is separated from the property of the fiduciary, trustor, or trustee or, in appropriate cases the recipient of any remaining property. Trusts cannot be used to modify the inheritance law since the Civil Code forbids the imposition of conditions and restrictions on the inheritance share attributable to heirs (ascendants, descendants and surviving spouse).

[171] Investment banks are corporations whose purpose is to promote investment in general, both in the country and abroad, whether as direct investors or as intermediaries between investors and entrepreneurs requiring capital. They cannot receive deposits from the public, make loans or grant contingent credits and, therefore, do not have credit portfolios.

[172] The municipal savings and loan banks mainly finance micro and small companies.

[173] In the case of a banking syndicate, a group of banks will jointly lend money to a specific borrower. A syndicate of banks is not a permanent entity but is formed specifically to carry out difficult, risky or large-scale operations.

6.5.3. Financing Limits

[174] In the case of loans to foreign companies, the credit, investment and leasing that a financial institution will grant to the relevant foreign company cannot exceed the equivalent of 5% of the net worth of such company. This rate could be raised to 10% of the net worth of the foreign company only if the latter can grant one of the following guarantees for an amount equivalent at least to the excess over the first limit (5%):

(a) Mortgage.
(b) Shares or bonds issued by a company, which are quoted on the stock exchange and over whose quality and prestige there is a pronouncement issued by a specialized and accredited institution of the relevant country.

[175] Exceptionally, the indicated limits of 5% and 10% respectively may be raised, as appropriate, to the equivalent of 30% of the effective net worth of the company, as long as the company obtains any of the following warranties/guarantees in respect of the excess:

(a) Cash deposits in-house, effected specifically for this purpose.
(b) Guarantees, securities and other obligations issued by a bank under the Agreement on Reciprocal Payments and Credits (celebrated between the Central Banks of the member countries of the – ALADI), or granted by a foreign first-class bank.

[176] In the case of loans to local companies, the companies within the financial system cannot grant, for or on behalf of the same natural or legal person, directly or indirectly, loans, investments or contingent payments exceeding the equivalent of 10% of its net worth.

[177] This limit is applicable to all kinds of financing and investment, except for bonds guaranteeing the subscription of contracts deriving from public tender, which are subject to a limit of 30%.

[178] The limit of 10% can be raised to the equivalent of 15% of its net worth as long as the company obtains any of the following warranties/guarantees in respect of the excess:

(a) Mortgages.
(b) Pledges involving legal or physical delivery.
(c) Warrants.
(d) Bills of lading and waybills which have been subject to endorsement or assignment (only applicable for financing imports).
(e) Guaranty trust over the goods referred to above.

6.5.4. Securities

[179] In accordance with the Peruvian regulation, there is no problem for a foreign lender to take security over a local property regardless of whether it is movable or not. In the case of guarantees over immovable property, the security must be in the form of a mortgage.

[180] If the property is located in Peru, the mortgage must be executed before a public notary who issues a public deed. Perfection of the collateral requires its filing in the Real Estate Property Registry in the jurisdiction where the property is located. If there is a breach of the underlying obligation, the secured party may commence a summary proceeding for the foreclosure of the property and collect on the debt from the proceeds of the sale.

6.5.5. Control over the Transfer of Funds

[181] There are no problems in transferring funds abroad; however, if the transfer is equal to or higher than USD1 000 or PEN3 500, the transaction must be completed through the intermediary of a bank (e.g., the company must proceed via an account in a bank of the domestic financial system in order to effect the necessary payments).

[182] It is possible that the bank may require the signing of a sworn statement explaining the reason(s) for the transaction.

6.5.6. Offshore Bank Accounts

[183] Peruvian regulation does not prohibit companies from having offshore bank accounts. However, companies operating abroad with these funds will not be able to deduct the associated expenses for income tax purposes.

6.5.7. Exchange Control

[184] Peruvian monetary policy has not established any exchange control or currency regulations. The Central Reserve Bank of Peru does not manipulate currency changes or establish rigid exchange rates.

[185] Notwithstanding the above, the Central Reserve Bank of Peru does on certain occasions intervene in the exchange market in order to avoid abrupt fluctuations. This control is effected by the withdrawal of foreign currency from the market through the purchase of foreign currency. The Central Reserve Bank of Peru also intervenes in the opposite way (i.e., it intervenes in the exchange market by selling foreign currency, thereby injecting more of this currency into the market).

7. SPECIFIC ISSUES OF COMPANY/SECURITIES LAW MERGERS

[186] There are two different types of merger provided for in the Peruvian Companies' Law:

(1) merger by integration, which implies that two or more companies integrate into the merging company, thereby creating a new company; and
(2) merger by absorption, whereby one or more companies are incorporated into the surviving company.

A company which is merged by integration is dissolved but not liquidated.

Once the regulations on merger control mentioned in section **[242]** come into force, these regulations will have to be observed.

[187] In its initial phase, the merger procedure involves the creation of a merger agreement proposal/project, which is prepared by the companies involved in the merger. This proposal should contain the valuation criteria used for the determination of the exchange ratio between the shares of the companies involved in the merger.

[188] This merger agreement should be approved by the respective boards of directors or administration of each company by majority vote. The merger must then be approved at the shareholders' meeting or assembly of each of the companies involved. The call to the shareholders' meeting or to the assembly must be published in the Official Gazette at least ten days prior to the meeting. Each company must disclose the following documents to its shareholders, partners, bondholders and other creditors:

- the merger agreement proposal/project;
- the latest audited financial statements of the respective companies;
- the shareholders' agreement and by-laws of the merging company; and
- the relationship between the main shareholders, directors and administrators of each of the companies involved in the merger.

[189] In order for the merger to be legally valid, it must be registered in the Peruvian Public Registry. Registration of the merger results in the extinction of the companies absorbed or integrated. The merger agreement gives the relevant shareholders or partners the right to withdraw.

[190] The creditor of any of the participating companies in the merger has the right to file an opposition to the merger. The term allowed for exercising the right to oppose expires thirty days after the last publication communicating the merger. The opposition is effected by means of a summary trial. In the meantime, the merger agreement is suspended until the company pays off the relevant creditors or guarantees the payment.

7.1. Spin-Offs

[191] A spin-off entails the transfer of all or part of a company's assets to one or more companies already in existence or formed for the purpose. If all the company's assets are transferred, the transferring company will be extinguished. If only part of the assets is transferred, the transferring company is not extinguished but must reduce its capital. The rights and obligations of the spin-off (transferring) company will be allocated proportionately to the company receiving the assets.

[192] To spin off a company, it is necessary to comply with the same requirements established by law or by the by-laws to modify the shareholders' agreement or the by-laws. Spin-off transactions are subject to similar rules as those applied to mergers, including the right of the shareholders to withdraw, the right of creditors to oppose the spin-off, the registration of the spin-off with the public registry and the requirement for a formal spin-off agreement proposal/project.

7.2. Acquisition of Assets

[193] *Where* an acquisition is made by the purchase of assets of a company, such transaction will have to be approved by the shareholders' meeting of the selling company in cases where the book value of the assets in question exceeds 50% of the capital stock of the selling company.

[194] Note that, depending on the asset types, the registration of the transfer in the public registry or with relevant regulatory bodies may be required.

7.3. Security Interests

[195] There are two types of guarantees:

(1) Real guarantees – These include (i) a mortgage, which is applicable to real estate property, and (ii) a pledge, which is given in respect of movable property, assets, inventory and/or shares. In case of default, guarantors would be subject to the appropriate process in order to execute/enforce these guarantees and to satisfy the creditor's interest.
(2) Personal guarantees – In which the guarantor has the personal obligation to pay the relevant debt and to satisfy the creditor's interest.

[196] In this sense, these guarantees should be formalized in writing and registered under the public record (if the guarantee allows it). Under this scenario, all the guarantees referred to above are conventionally used in bank loans.

[197] Under the new Securities Guarantee Law, a pledge is a security interest. In this sense, the concept of a floating charge (as defined under the Peruvian Civil Code) has been repealed. Nonetheless, it is possible to incorporate a guarantee as collateral, guaranteeing the current and other future obligations assumed with the same creditor.

[198] Additionally, the concept of a 'Mortgage of Production Unit' is regulated in Peru's Civil Code. The Mortgage of Production Unit is based on considering as a single unit all of the property and goods that are used for the purpose of such economic exploitation. Within this kind of guarantee/mortgage, it is possible to include not only the physical premises of a specific industry but also all of the assets (including movables) that are part of the economic activity of that industry.

[199] Securities, mortgages and charges must be recorded in the Real Property Register if they are to be enforceable. The debts in question must be recognized by the National Institute for the Protection of Free Competition and Intellectual Property (INDECOPI), so if all the necessary requirements are fulfilled and these have been duly approved by the authority, there should be no major problem in enforcing the payment of such debts.

[200] There is an order of preference/priority in the payment of debts: salaries and social benefits owed to workers, unpaid contributions to private pensions system or public pension systems, the Benefit Fund and Social Safety Nets and other pension systems created by law, and the interests and costs that may arise from such contributions as well as contributions to Social Health Insurance including interests, costs and surcharges that they generate; and maintenance claims. These credits are preferential and come before secured creditors. The only way in which such sums may become ineligible for collection is that relevant requirements were not complied with before the due date, or that certification of conformity from the authority was not given before the due date. On the other hand, the other possibility is that the debtor could be in a situation where there are no more assets to repay the debt. In these circumstances, the 'suspect period' starts a year before the beginning of the insolvency proceedings. During this period, the debtor is presumed to have acted fraudulently and, therefore, all acts carried out by the debtor could be declared ineffective as the debtor may have tried to hide his assets or otherwise to make the recovery of the debts more difficult.

7.4. Costs and Fees

[201] A merger or a spin-off will involve notarial and registry costs, which will be determined on an ad valorem basis depending on the values involved in the transaction.

[202] Also note that if the acquisition is made by means of a tender bid under the Securities Market Law, the filing of the bid documents will require the payment of a fee to the SMV.

[203] The mere transfer of unlisted shares of a corporation does not involve registration procedures.

7.5. Dividends

[204] Dividends can be distributed only out of distributable profits.

[205] A corporation can create various classes of shares, some of which may give their holders preferential rights over dividends. However, the exercise of such preferential rights will still be subject to the existence of distributable profits.

[206] Before any distribution of dividends can be made, the legal reserve must be completed.

[207] The legal reserve is 10% of the net distributable profits and is mandatory in each fiscal year until an amount equal to 20% of the capital stock has been completed.

Also, the company's by-laws may establish statutory reserves which will have to be completed before any distribution of dividends.

Dividends can be distributed to both domestic and foreign shareholders.

7.6. Purchase of Own Shares

[208] A company can purchase its own shares in order to cancel them in a capital reduction procedure.

[209] The shares can be purchased without reducing the capital stock in the following cases:

(1) where it is done pursuant to a 'shareholders' meeting agreement' to increase the face value of the remaining shares;
(2) in the case referred to above, when the consideration for the purchase is composed of titles that grant their holders rights over distributable profits of the company;
(3) if the acquisition is made to mitigate a potential damage to the company, in which case the company may not hold the shares for a period longer than two years; and
(4) in circumstances where a shareholders' meeting resolves that the company will retain the shares for a period no longer than two years. In this case, the shares held by the company may not exceed 10% of the paid-up capital stock.

7.7. The Corporate Veil

[210] Under Peruvian law, the corporate veil will be pierced when there is a presumption or evidence of fraud (e.g., on the corporation's insolvency, the siphoning of corporate funds by the shareholders, the absence of relevant corporate records, and where the corporate status is simply a facade for the shareholders' unlawful operations, tax evasion or other criminal acts).

7.8. Insolvency

[211] The main implication that may arise in the context of acquiring shares or businesses that have gone into insolvency is the risk that these may prove irrecoverable. This is because the insolvent company has to undergo an insolvency proceeding, pursuant to which shareholders would rank last for the collection of their debts. In the case of buying a company in insolvency, the insolvency proceeding may result in an order to pay the debts owed to creditors, with the eventual possibility of a restructuring process of the company. Therefore, the risk of buying shares or a business that is insolvent at the time of purchase may imply low chances of deriving incomes and profits from the transaction.

7.9. Choice of Law

[212] Choice of law and arbitration clauses is permitted and enforceable in Peru.

[213] In order to enforce foreign judicial rulings or foreign arbitral awards, it is necessary to follow a process of foreign resolution recognition before the local courts, a process called 'exequatur'.

7.10. Due Diligence

[214] The following are the main aspects to be reviewed and considered during due diligence procedures for total/partial acquisitions or mergers.

7.11. Corporate

7.11.1. Good Standing

[215] It is necessary to confirm that the target company is in good standing according to Peruvian Companies' Law and whether it has complied with formal corporate obligations and corporate governance rules. In that sense, it would be necessary to review the following documents:

- Copies of the corporate books of the company (shareholders/partners' meeting minute book and board of directors' minute book, as the case may be).
- Company's electronic record issued by the public registry.

7.11.2. Articles of Association and By-Laws

[216] It is important to review the following:

- Quorum and voting rights: This is especially important when the transaction is a partial acquisition.
- Limitations on the transfer of shares: To comply with all formalities established for the transfer of shares and to avoid any nullity actions.
- Dividends policy (important in partial acquisitions).

7.11.3. Shareholders' Agreements

[217] According to Peruvian Companies' Law, shareholders may enter into shareholders' agreements with other shareholders or third parties in respect of several provisions regarding the company and/or the shares. It is important that, although the company's by-laws prevail over any shareholders' agreement, any shareholders' agreement be reviewed, especially in partial acquisitions.

7.11.4. Ownership of the Shares/Capital Structure

[218] It is necessary to review the shares' registry book of the target company so as to ensure that the shares are registered in the name of the seller(s) and that the shares are free and clear of liens and of judicial measures.

7.11.5. Management and Representatives

[219] By means of the electronic record of the company and its corporate books, a third party can obtain information about the members of the management of the company, as well as its representatives.

7.11.6. Financial Situation of the Company

[220] It is necessary to assess the company's financial statements in order to check that the company is not involved in a financial deficit situation, as established by Peruvian Companies' Law.

7.12. Contractual Matters

7.12.1. Review of the Main Contracts of the Company

[221] The most important contracts of the target's business should be reviewed. For that purpose, it is a common practice to establish a threshold with the client to determine, in advance, which contracts are going to be reviewed depending on the agreements' value. It is also important to review those contracts that, by their nature, are relevant and critical to the business (key agreements); such as concession contracts, main supplier contracts, main customer contracts, financing agreements, etc. We detail below some of the matters that should be taken into special consideration during the review:

- Main obligations.
- Events of default.
- Unusual exposures.
- Change of control provisions.
- Term and termination clauses.
- Arbitration clauses and jurisdiction.

7.13. Litigation

[222] It is important to obtain a list of the company's judicial, arbitration and administrative procedures. Likewise, it is necessary to obtain a description of each threatened or pending claim, lawsuit, arbitration or investigation involving a claim against the company, any subsidiary or any of their respective officers or directors.

7.14. Collateral and Guarantees Granted by the Company

[223] It is important to review any collaterals granted by the company and the obligations which they involve. In this respect it is necessary to obtain information regarding all mortgages, liens, pledges, security interests, charges, guarantees, standby letters of credit or other encumbrances to which any property (real or personal) of the company is subject and all related material documentation and assets.

7.15. Property

7.15.1. Real Estate Property

[224] It is necessary to review the target company's real estate property. Such information can be obtained by reviewing the following information:

- The public deeds of transfer is a way of demonstrating title to property when, for example, it is not possible to register such right with the public registry, among other circumstances. Also, it is important to review the transfer public deeds since these include all the details of the transfer, which are usually not included in the public registry (the registration entry only includes a summary containing the essential points of the transfer).
- The real estate property's electronic record, which can be obtained for an administrative fee in the public registry offices.

- All purchase agreements, option agreements, rights of first refusal and other contracts creating rights in the property to be transferred.
- In extreme cases where there is no information either in the public registry or in transfer deeds, other elements such as the payment receipts for municipal taxes over the real estate property could be useful, but do not necessarily guarantee a firm property right.

7.15.2. Other Goods

[225] A list of all the company's assets and goods (of a value higher than the threshold established for the purpose of the due diligence exercise) should be obtained from the target company, including the corresponding documents of title. Should the goods be subject to registration in the public registry (such as vehicles) the electronic record should also be obtained.

7.16. Industrial Property

[226] Registration certificates in respect of all intellectual property, including but not limited to trademarks, service marks, trade names, slogans, logos, copyrights, patents, domain names owned or used by the company, including copies of the certificate or document evidencing its ownership or use.

[227] Copies of all applications filed for registration of intellectual property: (i) owned or used by the company; (ii) which the company wishes to own or use; (iii) which may be similar to the intellectual property owned or used by the company.

[228] A detailed description of all intellectual property proceedings, oppositions or litigation filed by the company or against it and copies of all software-related agreements.

7.17. Insurance

[229] It is important to assess the scope of the insurance coverage, as well as to ensure that the main assets of the company are covered by a corresponding insurance. In this respect the due diligence request list should include all insurance policies.

7.18. Regulatory Matters

[230] Relevant regulatory matters will depend on the industry sector of the target company. In any case, the company must provide its licences, authorizations, as well as information regarding any concession held, including pending permits, or administrative actions that the company may have before the relevant regulatory authorities, including permits over the use of natural resources, when applicable.

7.19. Labour Matters

[231] The following information should be reviewed.

7.19.1. Labour Information

[232] This section includes the basic labour information of the company:

- A list of employees, a review of the payrolls and a review of the category frames that determinate the salaries.
- A description of the employees benefit plans, including pension and profit sharing plans, bonus plans, deferred compensation plans, group insurance plans, major medical plans and welfare plans (including a description of any changes in these plans proposed, agreed upon, or under consideration).
- A description of any terminated pension plans.
- A description of any and all pending and threatened litigation, claims, grievances, actions, or proceedings, whether judicial, arbitral, or administrative, involving the company or its subsidiaries and relating to labour or employment matters, and all judgments, orders and decrees entered in any such actions during the past five years.

7.19.2. Unions

[233] A description of all collective bargaining agreements entered into between the company and any union, together with any addenda, supplements, memoranda of agreement, or changes thereto.

7.19.3. Employment Contracts Regime

[234] This section provides information about the characteristics of the hiring regime of the company:

- Identification of the key employees of the company, their hiring date, position and compensation for the last fiscal year.
- A summary of any significant employment agreements, whether oral or written, to which the company is a party.
- A summary of any significant services agreements and other agreements with independent contractors, whether oral or written, to which the company is a party. It is important to review these agreements because according to the principle of 'Reality Supremacy' established by Peruvian Labour Law, if in the relationship between the company and an independent contractor there are characteristics of a labour agreement, the Labour Authority may determine that the contractor should have been included in the company's payroll, and

the company will be obliged to pay the corresponding social benefits to suc contractor, as a new employee.

- A summary of any significant compensation and non-compensation agree ments and any confidentiality and trade secret agreements to which the com pany or its key employees are party to and a summary of the manner in whic such agreements are used.
- A review of the terms and conditions of the key employees' contracts, in orde to determine the existence of possible contingencies if terminated (e.g. golden parachute agreements).

7.20. Tax Matters

[235] In addition to the accounting due diligence, the tax matters due diligenc should include a review of the company's compliance with tax returns for timeli ness and delivery to appropriate tax authorities.

[236] It should also identify and describe any tax disputes, deficiency claims, pas or continuing audits with or by local or national taxing authorities.

7.21. Environmental Matters

[237] If the company develops projects that may have an impact on the environment, according to Peruvian Legislation it is necessary to check the relevant environmental certificate(s). In that context the relevant environmental certificate should be reviewed, as well as evidence of compliance with the stipulations and obligations stated in such certificate.

[238] It is also important to review other authorizations, permits or licenses that may apply to the specific activity of the target company, such as water rights, certificates of inexistence of archaeological remains as well as certain agreements related thereto, including contracts with the owners of the surface land when the target company conducts operations over lands owned by third parties (which is the case in most energy and mining projects).

7.22. Additional Consideration

[239] It is advisable to conduct interviews with the company's internal legal staff, external lawyers and other available consultants for their assessment of legal, commercial, administrative or other significant contingencies of the company.

[240] Before, during and after the due diligence procedure, it would be advisable to corroborate and compare the due diligence findings, through interviews with the target company's management, in order to be aware of any different points of view.

[241] We also recommend extending this interview mechanism to external lawyers and other available consultants for their assessment of legal, commercial, administrative or other significant contingencies of the company.

7.23. Antitrust/Merger Control

[242] On 19 November 2019, the Peruvian Government issued the Emergency Decree No. 13-2019 that establishes a regime of prior control of mergers and acquisitions. This decree was published in the official gazette 'El Peruano'. At first, the decree was due to come into force on 20 August 2020. However, the Government approved the delegation of competence to the Executive Power to rule on certain matters, including the extension of the entry into force of this regulation due to the impact of COVID-19, as well as the modification of this regime (Statement of Reasons).

[243] In addition, the Ministry of Economy and Finance has issued through its webpage a draft related to the Regulation of the Emergency Decree No. 13-2019, in order to obtain comments and suggestions about such proposed regulation from the private sector, especially from strategic guilds as well as citizens. The regulation seeks to develop the details regarding the procedure undertaken by Indecopi as well as the requirements and specifications related to the minimum thresholds determining which particular operations may require a prior control before they take place.

[244] Meanwhile, concentrations regarding the power industry and electricity sector (Law No. 26876, Antimonopoly and Ant-oligopoly Law of the Electricity Sector) are still subject to a specific merger control; then such concentrations must obtain prior authorization by Indecopi. On the other hand, some other companies in particular sectors may require the prior approval of their regulators for the validity of the transfer of their shares and/or merger (e.g., banks and insurers).

8. OTHER RELEVANT LAWS AND DUE DILIGENCE ISSUES

[245] The Peruvian Criminal Code, enacted in 1991, establishes fourteen different actions which are regarded as bribery-related crimes involving public officials. Moreover, since 2018, Peruvian legislation now punishes bribery acts between private individuals, having incorporated two new crimes to our Criminal Code. The penalties for public officials who commit a bribery crime run between four and fifteen years of imprisonment. Together with imprisonment, the Criminal Code also includes other kinds of sanction against public officials who unlawfully commit corruption crimes, such as future disqualification from office as a public official.

[246] On the other hand, private agents who commit acts of corruption involving public officials can face an imprisonment sentence of three to eight years.

[247] With the sole exception of the action described in section 400 of the Criminal Code (which may be committed by both a public official and a private individual), only public officials can commit the crimes described above. However, sections 397, 397-A, and 398 of the Criminal Code establish criminal penalties for private individuals who offer or give bribes to a public official. Notwithstanding this, private individuals can be included in corruption investigations – whether as accomplices or instigators. First-grade accomplices or instigators face the same penalty as the author of the crime.

[248] Since several key corruption cases went public in the past few years, there is usually huge media coverage on newsworthy cases involving corruption. The government has been trying to implement effective measures to avoid corruption and to punish corruption cases. As part of these efforts, in the past decade specialized courts for corruption cases have been created and the New Criminal Proceedings Code, that was initially expected to enter into force gradually by stages (with Lima at the end), has been brought into force on a nationwide basis in order to speed up the prosecution of corruption crimes. In addition, in 2017, the State established that the most serious crimes of corruption will be imprescriptible.

[249] Despite all these efforts, corruption is still an endemic problem in the country, and it is hard to assess whether there has been any material improvement.

[250] The US Foreign Corrupt Practices Act (FCPA) and the UK Bribery Act have had some repercussions locally as all major entities are now usually very conscious of the importance of complying with these regulations. However, the impact is felt most appreciably in the prevention efforts these entities carry out. No public cases of investigations for failure to comply with the FCPA or the UK Bribery Act have come into the spotlight, with the exception of the construction club case, more specifically *Odebrecht*.

[251] The corruption actions sanctioned by the Peruvian Criminal Code are as follows.

Passive Proper Bribery

[252] Section 393° of the Criminal Code provides for imprisonment of at least five years, and up to eight years, for a public official who accepts or receives a donation or any other advantage or benefit to carry out an act in violation of his duties or as a consequence of having failed to carry out his duties.

[253] If the public official directly or indirectly requests a donation, gift, promise or any other advantage to carry out or not to carry out an act in violation of his duties, he will be subject to imprisonment for six to eight years.

[254] If a public official, by threats of non-action or illegal action, imposes conditions on the performance of his duties in the form of a donation or benefit, he will be subject to imprisonment for at least eight years, but not longer than ten years.

[255] In these three cases, the individual found guilty is also subject to be dismissed from his office as well as to be disqualified from eligibility for public office or for work for a public agency.

[256] As in all corruption cases, proof of an illegal agreement between a public official and a private citizen is a necessary element of the crime.

International Passive Bribery

[257] Section 393º-A of the Criminal Code lays down that a public official or functionary from a foreign country or from an International Public Organization who directly or indirectly accepts, receives or requests a donation, promise, or any other benefit to do or not to do an act in the exercise of his official functions, in violation of his duties, or who accepts them as a result of having failed to comply with his obligations, in order to obtain or retain a business or other unlawful benefit in the conduct of international economic activities will be punished by imprisonment of five to eight years.

Passive Improper Bribery

[258] Section 394º of the Criminal Code lays down that a public official who accepts or receives a donation, promise or other benefits in order to carry out an action that is part of his regular duties will be punished by imprisonment of four to six years.

[259] In order for section 394º to apply, the payment, donation or benefit must be offered to the public official only to facilitate the fulfilment of his regular duties. Therefore, the mere fact of receiving the payment is illegal, as the payment is not conditioned on violation of the public official's duties.

[260] Furthermore, section 394 of the Criminal Code also provides a higher potential sentence for a public official who requests gifts, promises or any other benefit in connection with his duties. In this case, the potential jail sentence is between five and eight years.

[261] As in previous cases, the illegal agreement between the public official and the private citizen is a critical element in the proof of the crime.

Jurisdictional Passive Bribery

[262] Section 395º of the Criminal Code provides for a sentence of imprisonment between six and fifteen years for judges, prosecutors, arbitrators, experts, members of an Administrative Tribunal or other public officials with similar duties, who by any means accept or receive a donation, promise or any other advantage or benefit that is intended to influence a decision under their jurisdiction.

[263] If any such public official requests a bribe (donation, promise or any other advantage or benefit), then the individual found guilty of this crime would be facing an imprisonment term that could range between eight and fifteen years.

[264] As with the crimes referred to earlier, the individual found guilty is also subject to be dismissed from public office and/or to be disqualified for eligibility for public office or for work for a public agency.

Passive Proper Bribery in the Exercise of the Police Function

[265] Section 395-A° of the Criminal Code regulates a sentence of imprisonment between five and ten years for members of the National Police, who by any means accept or receive a donation, promise or any other advantage or benefit to carry out an act in violation of their duties or as a consequence of having failed to carry out his duties.

[266] If any such member of the National Police requests a bribe (donation, promise or any other advantage or benefit), then the individual found guilty of this crime would be facing an imprisonment term between six and ten years.

[267] The member of the National Police that condition the fulfilment of their duties to the delivery or promise of a donation or any other advantage will be sanctioned with imprisonment between eight and twelve years.

Passive Improper Bribery in the Exercise of the Police Function

[268] Section 395-B° of the Criminal Code regulates a sentence of imprisonment between four and seven years for members of the National Police, who by any means accept or receive a donation, promise or any other advantage or benefit to carry out or omit an act that is part of their regular duties.

[269] If any such member of the National Police requests a bribe (donation, promise or any other advantage or benefit) to perform or omit an act that is part of his regular duties, then the individual found guilty of this crime would be facing an imprisonment term between five and eight years.

Passive Corruption of Auxiliary Jurisdictional Personnel

[270] Section 396° of the Criminal Code also applies similar prohibitions on judicial clerks and court assistants and fixes penalties of five to eight years of imprisonment for infringers.

[271] The Criminal Code also establishes criminal penalties for any person who offers or gives a bribe to a judge, a prosecutor, arbitrator, expert, assistant of the court, etc. A higher penalty is imposed under section 398 of the Criminal Code if the person who offers the bribe is a lawyer.

Illegal Advantage of Public Position

[272] According to section 399° of the Criminal Code, a public official or public servant, who is found guilty of improperly having an interest, directly or indirectly, in any contract or operation in which he has participated by reason of his duties, should be punished by imprisonment of four to six years as well as by prohibition from working as a public functionary in the future. It is irrelevant, for the purposes of this provision, whether the public official takes the interest for his own benefit or for the benefit of a third party.

[273] The individual found guilty is also subject to be dismissed from his office as well as to be disqualified from eligibility for public office or for work for a public agency.

Traffic of Influences

[274] Section 400° of the Criminal Code lays down that a person who is found guilty of using his influence or who purports to have influence in order to receive, or to cause somebody to give or promise to give a donation or any other advantage or benefit to himself or for the benefit of a third party, by offering to intercede with a public official whom he knows or claims to know, and who is or is going to be involved in a legal case (judicial or administrative) should be subject to a sentence of imprisonment of four years and up to six years.

[275] The individual found guilty is also subject to be dismissed from his office as well as to be disqualified from eligibility for public office or for work for a public agency.

Illegal Enrichment

[276] Section 401° of the Criminal Code punishes any public official or public servant who is found guilty of unlawfully increasing his wealth (assets) during the course of his duties and establishes a potential imprisonment sentence of five to ten years.

[277] If the public official or public servant has held senior management positions in State institutions or State enterprises or is subject to political impeachment, he may be subject to imprisonment for ten to fifteen years.

Corruption Crimes Committed by Private Individuals

[278] With the sole exception of the action described in section 400° of the Criminal Code (which may be committed by both a public official and a private individual), only public officials can commit the crimes described above. However, sections 397°, 397°-A, 398° and 398°-A of the Criminal Code establish criminal penalties for private individuals who, as we have explained, offer or give bribes to a public official.

Active Bribery

[279] Section 397° of the Criminal Code provides for an imprisonment sentence of four to six years for an individual who by any means offers, gives or promises a donation, promise, advantage or any kind of illegal benefit in order to carry out an action in conflict with his duties.

[280] Therefore, an individual found guilty of providing, offering or promising to give a bribe to a public official will be subject to imprisonment for four to six years.

[281] On the other hand, if the action described in the previous paragraph is conducted in order to get the public official to carry out an action that is part of his duties, he will be subject to a penalty of at least three and up to five years of imprisonment.

[282] According to this provision of the Criminal Code, facilitation payments are strictly prohibited in Peru and moreover are considered an act of bribery, and the offender may be held criminally responsible according to the provisions explained above.

Transnational Bribery

[283] According to section 397°-A, an individual found guilty of giving, offering or promising to give a bribe (donation, promise or any other advantage or benefit) to a public official of a foreign country or of an international public agency in order to get him to carry out or to omit acts that are part of his regular duties, in order to obtain or retain a business or any other illegal advantage, should be punished with imprisonment of at least five and up to eight years.

Jurisdictional Active Bribery

[284] According to section 398°, any individual found guilty of offering, giving or promising an advantage or benefit to a judge, prosecutor, arbitrator, expert, or member of an Administrative Tribunal, with intent to influence a decision under their competence should be punished by imprisonment of five to eight years.

[285] When a bribe is given or offered to court clerks, judicial clerks, witnesses or interpreters, the infringer should be punished by imprisonment of at least four years, but not longer than eight years.

[286] Finally, if the person who gives or offers a bribe is a lawyer or belongs to a law firm, he should be subject to a sentence of five to eight years.

[287] In such cases, any individual found guilty by a court may also be prohibited from practising their profession, commerce or industry and will also cease to be eligible for public duties.

Active Bribery Concerning Police Function

[288] According to section 398°-A, any individual found guilty of offering, giving or promising an advantage or benefit to a member of the National Police, with intent for the officer to perform or omit an act in violation of their duties should be punished by imprisonment of four to eight years.

[289] When a bribe is given or offered or promised to members of the National Police, for the officer to perform or omit an act that is part of his regular duties, the infringer should be punished by imprisonment of at least three years but not longer than six years.

8.1. Autonomous Liability of Legal Entities for Corruption, Money Laundering and Financial Crimes of Terrorism

[290] Effective since January 2018, the Law No. 30424 establishes the autonomous liability of legal entities involved in crimes of transnational active bribery, active bribery, jurisdictional active bribery, terrorism financing, money laundering, simple and aggravated collusion and traffic of influences. Under this law, legal entities can be investigated, processed and sanctioned autonomously and independently of any criminal prosecution against their representatives, managers, executives or employees for the commission of the mentioned crimes.

[291] The law and its regulation establish that legal entities may develop and implement a crime prevention system in the entity in order to mitigate and ideally avoid the commission of crimes within that entity. Having an effective prevention system in force will serve to exempt the entity from liability in the case of a criminal investigation for the crimes referred to above. Sanctions that could be imposed in these cases start from fines and go all the way up to the dissolution of the entity.

[292] In this sense, the regulations of the law referred to above, approved through Supreme Decree No. 002-2019 which has been in force since January 2019, establish and develop the content, standards and minimum requirements that the prevention system should have. The companies should take steps to implement these aspects on the basis of self-regulation. The minimum requirements are identification, evaluation and mitigation of the relevant risks; designation of a prevention officer, implementation of a whistleblowing process, periodic communication and facilitation of the system, and continuous evaluation and monitoring of the prevention system.

[293] In circumstances where there is an investigation of the relevant crimes, the prosecutor can request the Superintendence of the Stock Market to issue a technical report analysing the implementation and functioning of the prevention system. This report will be important for the prosecutor to decide if the implemented prevention system is sufficient to exempt the legal entity from responsibility.

8.2. Criminal Law Against Money Laundering

[294] Peru has strict regulations regarding the prevention systems which most major entities are obliged to adopt. In this sense, through Law No. 27693 the Peruvian Finance Intelligence Unit (UIF-PERU) was created to receive, analyse, treat, evaluate and transmit information to detect money laundering and/or terrorism financing and therefore help in the implementation of a prevention system for crimes of money laundering and terrorism financing.

[295] This law listed the legal entities regarded as obligated by the law and which are forced (among other things) to implement a prevention system, to have a compliance officer and to report suspicious operations. These obligations are being imposed on more and more sectors of industry and commercial agents.

[296] The Financial Intelligence Unit is in charge of analysing all the information provided by parties subject to these obligations and is in charge of filing criminal complaints with the Prosecutor's Ministry in those cases where the commission of a crime is suspected.

[297] Additionally, the Regulation of Law No. 27693 which was issued through Supreme Decree No. 20-2017 applies to the obligated subjects the regulations established by Resolution SBS No. 789-2018 issued by the Superintendence of Banking and Insurance. These regulations establish that the obligated subjects should implement procedures in their prevention system to identify and mitigate risks of the commission of the relevant crimes. This includes (among other things) a Risk Prevention and Management Manual, a Code of Conduct, due diligence procedures, capacitation, registration of operations and suspicious operations and the designation of a compliance officer.

[298] The Criminal Law against Money Laundering (Legislative Decree No. 1106) establishes that the following actions constitute criminal offences.

Conversion and Transfer Acts

[299] According to section 1 of this legislation, any person who transforms, converts or transfers money, goods or profits from an illegal source of which he is aware or ought to be aware will face imprisonment of eight to fifteen years if the action is carried out with intent to avoid the identification of the origin of the assets or their seizure.

Hiding and Holding Acts

[300] Section 2 of the regulation establishes imprisonment sentences for any individual who acquires, uses, stores, administers, stewards, receives, hides or keeps in his power money, goods or profits from an illegal origin (of which he is aware or ought to be aware) with intent to avoid the identification of its origin or its seizure.

Transport, Import or Export of Money or Securities from an Illegal Source

[301] Section 3 of the Decree establishes imprisonment of eight to fifteen years for any individual who transports money or securities from an illegal source within Peruvian territory with the objective of avoiding its identification or seizure. The same sanction will be faced by anyone who imports or exports such money or securities to or from the country.

Failure to Report Suspicious Operations or Transactions

[302] The law provides sanctions of four to eight years of imprisonment to any individual who, being obliged by law, fails to comply with their professional duties or functions by intentionally omitting to communicate to the relevant authority suspicious transactions or operations which they had detected or of which they had become aware.

[303] If the omission is not intentionally conducted but is done with gross negligence, the individual would face imprisonment of one to three years.

Refusal to Provide, Delay in Providing or Falseness of the Information Provided

[304] Any individual who refuses to provide or delays the provision of information to the competent authority, relating to a current investigation or a judgment for money laundering, or who intentionally provides inexact or false information will face imprisonment of two to four years.

[305] If the action is carried out within an investigation for money laundering related to illegal mining, or to a criminal organization, or if the value of the goods involved is higher than UIT500, the period of potential imprisonment will be between three and five years.

[306] Finally, the law provides a limited amount of circumstances that may be regarded as extenuating.

8.3. Environmental Considerations

[307] The applicable environmental regulations will depend on the target industry, and on the level of environmental impact that the activities of the participant(s) in the transaction may cause. However, in general terms, the following environmental aspects may be regarded as applicable to any and all industries that cause an environmental impact.

8.4. Environmental Impact Instruments

[308] According to Law No. 27446, the National System of Environmental Impact Evaluation Law and its regulations, any activities that may cause an environmental impact should produce an environmental instrument, to be approved by the appropriate authority. Currently, the authorities responsible for approving environmental instruments are the National Service of Environmental Certification for Sustainable Investments (SENACE) and the sectorial authorities within the scope of their respective competences.

[309] The applicable environmental instrument varies depending on the anticipated level of environmental impact, according to the following criteria:

(a) Environmental Impact Declaration (DIA): This instrument applies to projects where the environmental impact is expected to be low.
(b) Semi-detailed Environmental Impact Study (EIA-sd): This instrument applies to projects where the environmental impact is expected to be moderate.
(c) Detailed Environmental Impact Study (EIA-d): This instrument applies to projects where the environmental impact is expected to be high.

[310] In addition, for those cases in which the relevant activities were initiated prior to the enactment of the environmental law, the applicable environmental instrument would be the Environmental Management Adaptation Program (PAMA). In this instrument, the company undertaking the project proposes a plan to conform over time the business activities to the enacted environmental laws currently in place.

[311] Peruvian regulations also mandate the approval of a closing plan/abandonment plan, in which the company which undertakes the relevant business also regulates the activities to be carried out on closure, in order to restore, so far as practicable, the environmental status which was obtained prior to undertaking the project. Please bear in mind that these activities are not only applied when terminating the relevant business but also are carried out: (i) throughout the development of the project; (ii) at the end of the project; and (iii) even after the project has finished. In order to ensure that these obligations will be duly performed, companies usually grant collateral for the value of the activities to be carried out, usually in the form of bank bonds or the incorporation of trusts.

8.5. Relationship with Communities

[312] In the process of obtaining the environmental impact instrument, it is necessary to request the opinion of the communities that may be affected by the project. This is done by a number of different means, including suggestion boxes, surveys, workshops, public audiences, among others.

[313] In addition, when the project could affect the ancient culture and traditions of an ancestral community, the government should undertake a prior consultation with the said communities, in order to establish the community's perspective regarding the pros and cons of the project. The opinion of the ancestral community in this regard is not mandatory unless the community rejects a project that could involve the relocation of that community.

[314] A third kind of relationship with communities will arise in those cases where the project needs a portion of land owned by a rural or native community. In these cases, the company undertaking the project will need to negotiate with the applicable community in order to obtain a right to use such portion of land for the project. In Peru, we have protective laws regarding the transfer of rights over community lands. This implies the existence of community assemblies that need special quorums and majorities to pass the resolutions required to transfer such rights.

It is very common for these assemblies to request not only compensation regarding the transfer of rights over the land but also other types of consideration, such as obligations to hire the community members as workers to undertake the project, to buy the goods produced by the community, or indemnification for the community in case of a breach of environmental laws.

8.6. Care of Archaeological Remains

[315] In order to develop the project, the company must first carry out an archaeological remains study over the areas of influence of the project. This study must be approved by the Ministry of Culture. If the study shows the existence of archaeological remains, the appropriate measures to avoid damage should be dealt with in the study to be filed with the Ministry of Culture. Usually, those findings do not impede the development of the project, but they do imply certain limitations that will depend on the characteristics of both the project itself and the archaeological remains found.

8.7. Water Rights

[316] In Peru there are three types of rights to use or take water: (i) licences, (ii) permits, and (iii) authorizations. Since the names of each of these respective water rights may lead to a different understanding, and to avoid confusion about the scope of the water right that each involves, we provide a brief definition below:

(a) Licence: This is a water right that allows the use of water resources for the purposes of the activity for which it was granted.
(b) Permit: This is a water right that is granted to remaining resources. In that sense, the right is subject to the existence of water remaining after those users with licences and authorizations have covered their respective assigned quota.
(c) Authorization: This is a water right that is granted to carry out investigations/studies, which does not necessarily imply that a licence will subsequently be granted.

[317] In addition, it should be noted that an authorization for the disposal of residual water may be needed.

8.8. Natural Protected Areas

[318] There are certain zones in Peru that are qualified as 'Natural Protected Areas' in order to preserve the environmental biodiversity. If the project is around one of these areas, special measures to avoid damage should be implemented.

Moreover, where the project is within a natural protected area, this does not neces sarily imply a veto against carrying out the project, since within natural protecte areas there are sub-areas with specific permitted activities, as set out below:

(a) Strict Protection Area – Only monitoring activities and, exceptionally, scien tific research.
(b) Wild Area – Monitoring and management activities, scientific research; a well as educational and recreational activities that do not involve the use o motorized vehicles.
(c) Touristic and Recreational Area – Educational, recreational and investigatio activities, allowing infrastructure to access and house visitors. Use of motor ized vehicles is allowed.
(d) Direct Gain Area – Allows the gain of wild flora and fauna, including fishin activities.
(e) Special Use Area – This type of sub-area has been subject to human activit prior to its qualification as a natural protected area. In addition, this qualifi cation is granted to sub-areas in which agricultural, fishing or other activitie could involve the transformation of the original ecosystem.
(f) Recovery Area – This is a transitory qualification, granted in order to repai significant damage which has been incurred by such sub-area.
(g) Historic-cultural Area – Allows infrastructure for visitors in order to promote investigation, education and recreational activities related to cultural values

8.9. Maximum Permitted Limits (LMP) and Environmental Quality Standards (ECA)

[319] All activities should respect the maximum emission limits of disturbances (such as noise, smog, solid waste, water residues, among others) to the air, soil and water.

[320] LMPs regulate such emission limits on a per individual basis; while ECAs regulate such limits in respect to the maximum emission that a particular area (river or portion of land, among others) can support.

[321] Businesses are responsible only for compliance with the LMPs, and not for the ECAs, unless such business is the only one that has emitted the disturbances in respect to a specific area, surpassing the maximum ECA allowed.

[322] As regards product safety laws, according to the Consumer Protection Code, Law No. 29571, no products or services offered in the market should lead, in normal or foreseeable conditions, to risks which are unjustified or which are not the subject of appropriate warnings, for the health and/or safety of consumers or their *goods*.

[323] Therefore, suppliers of such products or services should inform consumers, according to the nature of the relevant products or services, as to the best measures to keep the product in good condition, or for transport and delivery, warning the consumer of the relevant risks, as well as the correct way to use the product, and the steps to take in the event of harm or injury.

[324] Moreover, in the case of dangerous products or substances, when placed on the market, and/or when included as components within other products, such products should comply with relevant laws requiring packages that protect the health and safety of consumers, including (in an appropriately clear and visible manner) instructions for the use of the product and appropriate warnings as to its use.

[325] Warnings as to the risks and dangers that should be included according to law, in respect of certain products or services, or as to the foreseeable and non-foreseeable risks that may be detected after the product has been placed on the market, should comply with the following:

- The warning should be issued in due time, according to the severity of the situation, and the exposure/risk involved.
- The size and frequency of the warning should be adequate.
- The nature of the risk should be specified indicating if such risk affects the life or health of the consumer.
- The measures required to avoid risk or to reduce its effects. The warning should explain how to fix those problems in a clear and easy way.
- An additional source of information should be included, free of charge and easily accessible by consumers, where further information can be located as to warnings about the risks and dangers of the product, indicating a toll-free contact number or its location. Such information should also be provided immediately to INDECOPI.

[326] The above regulation also includes product liability. According to the definition provided by law, liability will arise in respect of those products that are not safe to use, taking into consideration relevant circumstances such as:

(a) The product design.
(b) The way in which the product has been placed on the market, including its appearance, the use of any trademark, any advertisement related to the product, its method of use and warnings.
(c) The anticipated or predictable use of the product.
(d) The materials, content and condition of the product.

[327] In this regard, suppliers are liable for the damage caused to the physical integrity of the consumers or to their goods due to the failure of the products.

8.10. Intellectual Property Considerations

[328] According to Peruvian legislation (Decision 486 and Legislative Decree No. 1075), trademarks and patents are protected upon registration with the Peruvian trademark office (INDECOPI).

8.10.1. Trademarks

[329] The length of time from filing the trademark application to obtaining the certificate of registration is approximately four months if no opposition is filed. Registration is granted for a period of ten years, which is then renewable for ten years more and so on.

[330] The requirements for applying for the registration of a trademark in Peru are as follows:

- Applicant's name and domicile.
- Clear and complete description of the trademark.
- Samples of the logo if the trademark contains graphic elements, including its colours.
- List of products or services to be covered by the trademark and its international class pursuant to the Nice Convention.
- Power of attorney executed by a representative duly authorized by the applicant company. For registration purposes this document does not need any legalization, but for cancellations, withdrawal and renunciation of registration cases, this power will require legalization from all the appropriate authorities in the applicant's jurisdiction and finally by the Peruvian Consulate. This document may be filed within thirty days following the filing date of the application.

8.10.2. The Enforcement of Trademarks

[331] The trademark owner can take legal action against third parties for the unauthorized use of their registered trademarks and can request, for example:

- The cessation of all infringing acts.
- Withdrawal of all infringing products from the market.
- A prohibition against import or export of the infringing products.
- Destruction of the products, or the temporary or permanent closure of the business.

[332] Also a registered trademark owner can prevent third parties from registering trademarks and logos with similar characteristics to the ones they own, by filing opposition against such trademark applications. Additionally, the owner of a registered trademark can oppose trademark applications by filing Andean opposition, but only if the owner of the trademark (owns) has a registry in Bolivia, Ecuador or Colombia (Andean Community Countries).

8.10.3. Patents

[333] To be patentable, an invention must:

- Be novel.
- Involve an inventive step.
- Be capable of industrial application.

The following are not considered as inventions:

- Discoveries, scientific theories and mathematical methods.
- Any existing living being, existing in nature.
- Biological material, existing in nature.
- Natural biological processes.
- Literary or artistic works or any work protected by copyrights.
- Plans, rules and methods for the exercise of intellectual activities, games or economic commercial activities.
- The software or logic support, as such.
- Ways of presenting or displaying information.

[334] The information and documents required to file a patent application are:

(a) Applicant's name, nationality and domicile.
(b) Inventor's name, nationality and domicile.
(c) A complete description of the invention to be registered.
(d) A summary of the invention.
(e) Claims of the invention.
(f) Drawings of the invention, if any.
(g) A copy of the foreign application if priority rights are claimed. According to the Paris Convention, this document does not require any legalization.
(h) Power of attorney (which does not require any legalization).
(i) Deed of Assignment executed by the inventor(s) and the applicant, duly legalized by a Notary Public and the Peruvian Consulate.
(j) A copy of the Patent Cooperation Treaty (PCT) application, if applicable.

[335] In order to maintain the patent or the patent application in force, an annual fee should be paid to the competent authority, INDECOPI.

[336] A patent owner can prevent unauthorized third parties from making, selling, offering for sale, using, or importing for such purposes the patented product or process. The owner of a patent or of a patent application that is being processed can license third parties to exploit the invention it covers.

[337] In order to be protected a patent must be registered at the Department of Inventions and New Inventions of INDECOPI.

[338] The patent owner can take legal action for unauthorized use of the invention and can request, for example:

- The cessation of all infringing acts.
- Withdrawal of all infringing products from the market.
- A prohibition against import or export of the infringing products.
- Destruction of the products, or the temporary or permanent closure of the business.
- Publication of the guilty verdict and notification of interested parties at the infringer's expense.

[339] The protection of a patent lasts for twenty years from the date of filing the application for registration. After this period, the patent enters the public domain.

8.10.4. Industrial Designs

[340] Industrial design is the particular appearance of a product resulting from any combination of lines or colours, or any dimensional outward form, line, contour, form, texture or materials, without changing the destination or purpose of the product.

[341] Only new designs are capable of registration and their novelty will be analysed on a worldwide basis, not restricted to Peruvian territory.

[342] Designs are registered at the Department of Inventions and New Technologies of INDECOPI.

[343] The industrial design registry grants to a registered owner the exclusive right to exclude any third party from using the registered design. Therefore, the owner of a registered design can take legal action against third parties, preventing the fabrication, import, offer for sale, marketing or use in commerce of products that include or reproduce industrial designs.

[344] Protection lasts for ten years from the date of filing of the application in any of the Andean Community Country members.

8.10.5. Copyright

[345] All regulations in Peru related to Copyrights are regulated by Legislative Decree No. 822, also known as the Copyrights law.

[346] According to this regulation copyright subsists automatically from the date of creation; however, it can be registered with the Copyrights Office of INDECOPI, as a means of advertising registration and establishing priority.

[347] Protection lasts for the life of the author plus seventy years after the author's death. The author is entitled to enforce copyrights. The right can be enforced by initiating an infringement action at an administrative proceeding or by a criminal action if the facts are regarded as a crime.

[348] In relation to administrative proceedings, the penalties for breach include:

- A warning.
- A fine of up to UIT180.
- Temporary closure of the business for ninety days.
- Seizure of the goods.
- Permanent closure of the business.
- Publication of the guilty verdict and notification of interested parties at the infringer's expense.

8.10.6. Database

[349] Databases are protected in the same way as by copyright laws.

[350] With respect to the verification of intellectual property for due diligence purposes, this will depend on the number of relevant registries and intellectual property rights the relevant company owns. For due diligence purposes, a search at the Peruvian Trademark Office will be carried out in order to verify the information provided by the seller against that provided by the authority.

[351] Agents and distributors are not entitled to mandatory compensation or other indemnities on termination of their contracts unless agreed by the parties under the terms of those contracts.

[352] Notwithstanding the above, experience and Peruvian court precedents appear to indicate that during the performance of agency/distribution agreements, agents/distributors may obtain the right to be indemnified or to be compensated for a unilateral termination of the agreement on the part of the manufacturer, as long as the agent/distributor can prove that:

(a) it has made significant investments to carry out the agreement in the manner required by the manufacturer; and
(b) the manufacturer's behaviour and actions may have contributed to the belief or misled the agent/distributor into believing that its intention was to continue with the performance of the agreement or to encourage the latter to make significant investments.

[353] In view of the above, it is important to bear in mind that, although unilateral termination clauses offering no compensation to the agent/distributor are legally permitted in agency/distribution agreements pursuant to Peruvian Law, it is also necessary to take into account that the manufacturer's actions or behaviour must not encourage or mislead the agent/distributor to make investments to achieve the objectives of the agreement, because if the agreement is terminated, the distributor may allege that this is evidence of bad faith, in order to obtain an indemnity or compensation for the termination of the agreement.

[354] Please note that the agent/distributor seeking indemnification must prove both the damage and the amount of the said damage.

9. THE DUE DILIGENCE PROCESS

[355]

(1) Whether or not the seller is comfortable with the full due diligence investigation will depend, in our experience, on the type of seller. We find that sellers of companies with significant commercial experience of sophisticated transactions seem more comfortable with undertaking the due diligence procedure since they understand its necessity if the deal is going to get done. However, sellers of small or family companies seem more reluctant to deliver their companies' information for due diligence purposes,

particularly when they have not been exposed to transactions of this nature.

(2) In relation to property, it is a common practice to obtain from the sellers: (i) the certificates of title (understood as the registration of property), and (ii) the document that originates the registration process (such as the public deed). Furthermore, it is common to double check this information by investigation of public sources.

(3) Environmental audits are common, since liabilities arising from breach of environmental regulations may attach to the company that is being acquired, in addition to its management and administrators. The usual practice on environmental matters is to have a multidisciplinary approach to the due diligence process, which will include (together with the review of legal aspects) an assessment from a third-party engineering advisor as to compliance with environmental regulations.

(4) Both physical and virtual data rooms are commonly used. In recent years, the use of virtual data rooms has become more common than physical data rooms.

(5) Some specific legislative issues that may arise in the due diligence process include:

(a) *Agreements with rural/native communities for the transfer of their lands* – Peruvian legislation is protective of the rural/native communities, which sometimes results in difficulties – in both the negotiation and fulfilment of agreements with them. For example, according to law, special quorums and majorities are required in order to transfer rights over the community's lands.

In view of the above, regular assessment of the status of the relationship with rural/native communities would be advisable in order to verify that the performance of the agreement matches with the authentic current status of the community's interests.

It is common to have a multidisciplinary due diligence team to consider not only legal due diligence aspects but also a specialist assessment of the status of social relationships.

(b) *Search of judicial procedures* – In order to obtain information about judicial processes to which an individual/company may be party, it is necessary to search separately in all judicial districts, since there is no centralized search system. For this purpose it is normal to conduct the search at least in those judicial districts where the company carries on business, where its domicile is located, as well as in Lima downtown judicial districts.

(c) *Public registry searches* – The public registry search system could be improved, particularly in matters such as the search for real estate property by address as well as non-registered assets.

(6) In order to conduct an efficient due diligence procedure, we recommend to proceed as follows:

(a) Learn as much as possible about the business to be acquired, including administrative and technical aspects. This implies direct conversations with the management and visits to the administrative and operational premises (if possible).

(b) Define the key issues from the perspective of the business to be acquired, in order to address them correctly. This includes setting up a materiality threshold for the documents to be reviewed.
Key issues for review may also include possible synergies and cost efficiency strategies.

(c) Provide a clear executive summary of the key issues and main contingencies to be considered when acquiring the business (significant or lengthy information can be included as a schedule, exhibit or in other ways).

(d) It is essential to have a fluid and direct relationship with other due diligence investigators, such as financial advisors, technical advisors and, ultimately, other law firms (whether local or foreign), in order to deliver a coordinated report on all aspects of the due diligence.

(7) As regards the relationship between the due diligence findings and the imposition of contractual representations, warranties and indemnities, there are two alternative approaches:

(a) The first approach takes the view that there is no need to include representations and warranties and related indemnities in the relevant acquisition documents, since, in principle, the purchaser intends to obtain, for the purpose of due diligence, all the information it needs about the business and the sellers' activities, and to rely only on that information.

(b) The second approach states that representations and warranties, as well as the related indemnities on the part of the sellers, should be applicable since the due diligence exercise conducted by the purchaser is merely a supporting and informational document for the purchaser.

[356] Of course, there are a number of variants on these basic positions which are negotiated by the parties.

[357] Customarily, in our jurisdiction, acquisition agreements contain representations and warranties from the seller(s), with any exceptions to those representations being set out as exhibits to the acquisition documents. The indemnification mechanism usually arises out of particular exceptions for which the seller(s) are unwilling to accept the risk; an amount equal to the value of such exceptions to the representations and warranties is usually: (i) discounted from the purchase price; or (ii) placed into an escrow account.

[358] Representations, warranties and indemnities are widely used, accepted and enforceable in Peru. Usually, acquisition documents will follow the US format.

[359] Finally, please note that while it is customary to agree on arbitration to settle this type of issue, some parties tend to agree on specialist technical arbitrations for particular types of issue that may arise from a breach of any of the representations and warranties.

10. THE ROLE OF THE COURTS

[360] In Peru, we have two different jurisdictions with the same ability to resolve disputes, which are:

(1) the Judiciary, or the ordinary jurisdiction; and
(2) arbitration.

[361] The judicial system arrives at independent decisions for the resolution of cases in disciplinary, economic and administrative issues. The judiciary has three levels: The Supreme Court, various superior courts, and the lower courts. For very specific cases, below these are the judges of peace. The judicial system is organized according to Peruvian political divisions. The political organization of the country has been changed into several regions and districts. The extent and distribution of a decentralized government have been left to legislative mandate.

[362] Once the parties have enforced an arbitration agreement, a court can no longer rule on the matter. The arbitration agreement may be related to disputes which have already arisen as well as those that may arise in the future. The agreement must be in writing, whether by a clause inserted in a particular contract or as a separate arbitration agreement. If there is no previous agreement, it is understood that the arbitral agreement is formalized in writing once the parties participate in an arbitral proceeding without objecting to the arbitrators' competence.

[363] Investments, whether national or foreign, are currently highly encouraged. The judiciary is totally independent of other government powers.

[364] Most investments or contracts are submitted to arbitral jurisdiction. One of the main reasons for this is that it takes less time to solve a controversy by means of arbitration than by submitting the dispute to the judiciary, which could take, on average, five years.

[365] Injunctions can be requested both from the judiciary and in the context of Arbitration to the Arbitral Tribunal in order to ensure the enforceability of the judicial ruling or arbitral award.

[366] An injunction may be enforced within fifteen to thirty days, depending on the workload of the Judiciary or the Arbitral Tribunal.

[367] According to the law, a warranty has to be granted by the applicant in case the other party is (unjustifiably) caused harm as a result of the injunction granted. The necessity for such a warranty provides a useful deterrent for the party against whom the judgment is sought.

11. MERGER CONTROLS: ANTI-TRUST/ COMPETITION ISSUES

11.1. Control Law for Mergers and Acquisitions

[368] The Peruvian Government issued the Urgent Decree No. 13-2019, which establishes prior control for mergers and acquisitions, and which was finally published on 19 November 2019 in the official gazette 'El Peruano'. This law requires that in particular cases it will be mandatory to communicate with the relevant authority (Indecopi) and to obtain an authorization from it before carrying out a business operation involving a merger and/or acquisition. The objective of the law is to guarantee that such operations would not represent an anticompetitive practice within the Peruvian market. Thus, it seeks to promote economic efficiency in the markets for the welfare of consumers, since in certain cases, such operations could have a negative impact on the market and affect competition.

[369] However, given the COVID-19, and the declaration of the State of Emergency issued by the Peruvian Government, this law will not come into force until 1 March 2021 (the original date was 20 August 2020) and will remain in effect for five years. In this *sense*, from this date enterprises intending to carry out mergers or acquisitions (including the purchase of companies, joint ventures, classic mergers, among others) will be obliged to communicate in advance to Indecopi its intention to carry out a particular operation in order to obtain an authorization or clearance prior to implementing a merger agreement, when such operation involves one of the specific cases referred to in this law.

[370] This law will be applicable to all acts of concentration that produce effects in all or part of the national territory, including acts undertaken abroad that link, directly or indirectly, to any economic agent carrying on economic activities in Peru. Therefore, Article 5° of the Urgent Decree defines an act of concentration as one that involves a permanent transfer or change of control of a company or part of it, and which is generated as a consequence of the following operations:

- Mergers.
- Acquisitions.
- Joint Ventures: the constitution by two or more independent economic agents of a joint venture or any other similar contractual modality that involves the acquisition of joint control over one or several economic agents (which economic agent performs permanently the functions of an autonomous economic entity).
- The acquisition by an economic agent of direct or indirect control, by any means, of productive operating assets of other economic agents.

[371] Additionally, Article 6° of Urgent Decree No. 13-2019 establishes the following economic thresholds that may require companies to communicate with Indecopi regarding their potential operations and which must be met, concurrently:

(1) The total sum of the value of the annual sales or gross income in the country of the companies involved in the operation has reached, during the fiscal year prior to that in which the operation is notified, a value equal to or higher than 118 000 Tax Units (USD144 971 482, approximately).
(2) The value of the annual sales or gross income in the country of at least two of the companies involved in the operation have reached, during the fiscal year prior to that in which the operation is notified, a value equal to or higher than eighteen thousand (18,000) Tax Units each (USD 23 114 285, approximately).

[372] Concentration operations within the scope of the SBS, may be allowed to proceed if they obtain the authorization of Indecopi and SBS, each acting within the scope of their legal attributions. Likewise, the joint authorization of Indecopi and the SMV will be required for concentration operations of economic agents who have obtained an operating license from the SMV.

[373] The authorization is requested from the Technical Secretariat of the Free Competition Commission of Indecopi and, if it is denied, it can be appealed before the Court of Indecopi.

[374] The Commission will simply approve the concentration, or approve it subject to conditions, or refuse it, or continue with its evaluation for a further period of ninety working days. The final resolution of the Commission can be appealed to the Tribunal of Indecopi within fifteen days.

[375] Once the law on prior control of concentration operations enters into force, Law No. 26876 (Antimonopoly and Ant-oligopoly Law of the Electricity Sector) will be repealed.

[376] The Regulation of the aforementioned law must be issued in November 2020.

[377] In this regard, the Ministry of Economy and Finance has issued through its webpage a draft related to the proposed Regulation of the law, in order to obtain comments and suggestions about such regulation project from the private sector, especially from strategic guilds as well as citizens. The regulation seeks to develop the details regarding the procedure undertaken by Indecopi as well as the requirements and other specifications related to the thresholds, and which particular operations may require a prior control before they take place.

11.2. Scope of the Controls

[378] Meanwhile, only concentrations regarding the power industry and electricity sector (Law N° 26876) remain subject to a specific merger control; on implementation such concentrations will also have to obtain prior authorization by Indecopi. On the other hand, only transactions involving certain specific industries or economic sectors (i.e., banking and insurance; energy/power sector) are ruled by specific regulations and may require specific notifications or authorizations.

[379] It should be noted that concentration operations carried out before the law comes into force, will not be subject to prior control, except for those in the electricity sector, in accordance with the Antimonopoly and Anti-oligopoly of the Electricity Sector Law, Law No. 26876, which establishes the control of mergers and acquisitions by means of a notification to Indecopi before the date of change of control.

[380] A prior regulatory authorization is required in connection with the acquisition of a banking or insurance business. Whenever a person or entity acquires more than 10% of the capital stock of a bank or an insurance company, it will need to request and obtain the prior authorization of the Superintendence of Banking, Insurance and Pension Funds. Such authorization must also be requested and obtained by the transferor of the relevant shares.

[381] In the electricity sector, from an antitrust regulation perspective, the Law against Monopoly and Oligopoly in the Electrical Sector Law, Law No. 26876, provides for the control of mergers and acquisitions by means of a notification to the Indecopi before the date of the change. However, it should be pointed out that Indecopi has never rejected a request for concentration since the enactment of this law.

[382] In this regard, the only relevant case was an Indecopi Resolution where the Tribunal allowed an electric company's request for a merger with another company rendering the same services, but restricting their right to vote within the Committee of Economic Operation of the National Interconnected System (COES). COES is a nonprofit private entity with public capacity, whose decisions must be fulfilled by all electric agents. COES manages the security of electric energy supplied to more than 70% of the Peruvian population.

[383] Indecopi considered this to be a proportional and necessary solution since it ensured that the operation of COES in all its levels of decision would not respond to the particular interests of a specific company, but to the better operation of the electrical system, which would finally improve the conditions for competence, consumers, and electric energy users.

11.3. Anticompetitive Restraints

[384] It is common for the purchaser of a business to wish to prevent the vendor from taking advantage of the knowledge he has acquired to start a new competing business. It is possible for the purchaser to include in the purchase agreement a clause setting out a compromise from the vendor not to compete during a fixed period of time. In consideration of such a compromise in the purchase agreement, an additional payment can be added to the purchase price, in order to ensure that the vendor will respect the compromise.

[385] As regards employees, it is important to note that the labour chapter of the Peruvian Constitution aims to protect employees and promotes the freedom of work. It expressly states that labour agreements must not limit any employee's constitutional rights. Furthermore, pursuant to the Constitution, in cases of doubt about the effect of a regulation on employees' rights, the judge must interpret the regulation in favour of the employee. Accordingly, labour courts are always aiming to protect employees.

[386] Thus, a possible mechanism to deter the management team or key employees from leaving would be to offer compensation that would be paid against the compromise of the employee to stay for a reasonable period of time. Such compensation would have to be paid at the end of this period of time. Aside from this possibility, the employee is free to leave at any time; it is the responsibility of the company to create incentives in order to encourage him to stay.

[387] Additionally, it has to be underlined that any merger that allows a company to obtain a dominant position in the market would be under the scrutiny of the Free Competition Commission of Indecopi. The reason for such 'supervision' is related to the prohibition of abuse of dominant position under both the Peruvian Constitution and Peruvian Antitrust Law.

[388] The Free Competition Commission of Indecopi may sanction illicit collusive vertical practices when one of the companies involved has a dominant position. However, this kind of practice is analysed by reference to the rule of reason. Vertical practices are those undertaken by or between two or more competing businesses operating at different levels of the production or distribution chain in the market (e.g., a vertical agreement could be between a manufacturer, a distributor and a retailer). The most common cases are:

- Agreeing directly or indirectly to fix prices or other commercial conditions or services.
- Limiting or agreeing to act in concert on the control of production, distribution, technical development or investment.
- Agreeing on a division of customers, suppliers or geographical markets.
- Agreeing on product quality when this is not in accordance with national or international technical standards such as to negatively affect consumers.
- Applying in business relationships, unequal conditions for equivalent services that may put some competitors at a disadvantage relative to others.
- Subjecting the purchase of a product to the acceptance of additional services which have no relationship with the main contract.
- The unjustified and concerted refusal to satisfy demands for purchase or acquisition or offers to sell or provide products or services.
- A boycott in order to limit access to the market or the free exercise of competition by other companies.
- Signing, without proper justification, exclusivity, distribution or sales contracts.
- The establishment, agreement or coordination of (or abstention from) bids, tenders, or other means of contracting, or public acquisition as provided for in the applicable legislation, as well as public auctions and sales.

[389] This list of examples is not meant to be exhaustive but illustrative; the Free Competition Commission of Indecopi may regard as antitrust practices, other cases having equivalent effects. It is sufficient to prove that the practice has or may have an equivalent anticompetitive effect to any of the specific practices stated as examples in the law.

[390] However, having a dominant position in the relevant market and concluding (e.g.) an exclusive vertical distribution agreement, will not 'per se' be regarded as an infringement of the Peruvian Antitrust Law, because collusive vertical practices are 'relative prohibitions'. In other words, the Commission will apply the 'rule of reason' and will determine whether the advantages obtained by a company in the market are a consequence of superior efficiency in the use of resources or the result of illegal practices. This process allows the parties to defend themselves, demonstrating that their conduct does not generate any detrimental effect on the market and, therefore, on consumers.

[391] Bear in mind that Indecopi, whether or not one of the companies involved holds a dominant position in the relevant market, may also sanction as illegal horizontal agreements between competitors at the same level of production or distribution in the market, and where similar practices to those referred to above are engaged in.

[392] Competitors of the purchaser could denounce such practices to Indecopi, in order to trigger investigations and (where such practices are regarded as illegal) the imposition of fines.

[393] There are no individual or block exemptions provided for by law. To conclude, in order to be regarded as illegal, a collusive vertical practice requires that at least one of the companies involved must have a dominant position in the relevant market. On the contrary, a horizontal collusive practice may be regarded as illegal independently of the existence of a dominant position involving the companies concerned.

12. TAXATION ASPECTS

12.1. Nature of the Tax Regime

[394] We would characterize our jurisdiction as a relatively certain environment for tax purposes.

[395] In general terms, the tax rules are clear. However, there is an increasing tendency towards the sophistication of tax rules, especially those to avoid tax evasion.

[396] The Peruvian tax system is regulated by several statutes. Article 74 of the Peruvian Constitution of 1993 has established that all taxes have to be created, modified, or eliminated by law (or by Legislative Decree when the corresponding powers have been delegated by the Legislative Branch to the Executive Branch).

This premise is also applicable to tax exemptions and establishes the principles applicable to the tax law.

[397] The Tax Code is the main statute (law) which includes the principles guiding the application of taxes, as well as provisions concerning the nature of taxes, the powers/faculties of the Tax Administration, the Tax Court, tax proceedings and penalties.

[398] The most important taxes imposed on individual investors and companies are the following: (i) income tax; (ii) VAT; (iii) excise tax; (iv) customs duties; (v) real estate property tax; (vi) financial transactions tax; (vii) temporary tax on net assets; and (viii) social security contributions.

[399] On the other hand, Peru has entered into a number of 'Agreements to Avoid Double Taxation' (AADT's) which are in force within the Andean Community (Colombia, Ecuador and Bolivia), Chile, Canada, Brazil, Mexico, Portugal, Switzerland and the Republic of Korea.

[400] Certain procedures and tax rules are quite complex. The Peruvian Tax Administration (SUNAT) shows a tendency to aggressively enforce the tax regime in order to achieve its collection goals. The Peruvian government is also progressively adopting measures of the base erosion and profit shifting (BEPS) Plan in the domestic law as part of its aim to become a member of the Organisation for Economic Co-operation and Development (OECD).

13. LIABILITY TO TAX

[401] Peruvian resident business entities (companies, partnerships and any other structure used to conduct business, including resident partnerships, limited liability companies, taxable foundations and associations, as well as joint ventures maintaining accounting records independent from those of the relevant venturers) will be subject to taxation on their worldwide income. All of them will be subject to the same tax treatment.

[402] The results of their overseas transactions will be netted off and added to their domestic source net income, but only if they result in a net income (losses from tax havens cannot be netted off against foreign source income). Net losses from a foreign source cannot be offset against domestic source net income for income tax purposes.

[403] Non-resident business entities, on the other hand, are taxed on their Peruvian source income only. Likewise, branches and other permanent establishments of non-resident entities are taxed on their Peruvian source income only. The Peruvian Income Tax Law establishes rules in order to determine whether the benefits obtained qualify as Peruvian source income.

[404] The main taxes in Peru are the following: *Corporate income tax* – Peruvian domiciled corporations are taxable on their worldwide income. Despite the fact that branches and permanent establishments of non-domiciled corporations are considered domiciled taxpayers, they are taxed only on their Peruvian income. Nevertheless, they are subject to the same formal obligations (accounting, bookkeeping, filing of tax returns, etc.) as corporations.

[405] The results of the corporation's overseas transactions will be netted off and then added to their domestic source net income, but only if this results in a net income. It is important to highlight that losses from tax havens cannot be combined with foreign source income. Net losses from a foreign source cannot be netted off against domestic source net income for income tax purposes. The Peruvian Tax Law allows certain tax paid abroad to be offset against Peruvian income tax liability as a tax credit. Note that tax credit must be on the same income as is taxable in Peru.

[406] The net income obtained by domiciled corporations is considered as third-category income and is subject to a 29.5% tax rate.

[407] Expenses incurred during the fiscal year by domiciled corporations are generally deductible for tax purposes, provided that they are deemed necessary for obtaining third-category income as well as for maintaining the income source, unless deductibility is expressly prohibited by law (e.g., in the case of personal expenses, income taxes, fines, donations not complying with certain conditions, certain provisions or reserves, VAT and excise taxes, the transfer of property without consideration, expenses supported by invoices that do not fulfil the requirements established by the Invoices Regulations, among others). Peruvian source net losses may be applied against the annual net income in order to assess the income tax payable.

[408] *Value Added Tax (VAT):* This tax is applied to the consumption of goods and services rendered in Peru as follows: (i) local sales of goods; (ii) the rendering or use of services within the country; (iii) construction contracts; (iv) the first sale of real estate carried out by the constructor; and (v) the customs value of imported goods. The current VAT rate is 18%. The transfer of shares is not subject to the levy of VAT. The export of certain goods and services executed abroad are exempted from VAT, provided certain requirements are met.

[409] In order to determine the appropriate VAT due, the VAT credit has to be deducted from the monthly gross tax (meaning the amount resulting from the application of the VAT rate (18%) to sums derived from any transaction subject to this tax). On the other hand, the tax credit is the tax paid on the acquisition of goods, services and construction contracts or the payment for the importation of goods or for the utilization of services within the country rendered by non-residents.

[410] *Excise Tax (ISC):* The excise tax is levied on the local sale at manufacturer level and the import of goods such as fuels (gas, gas-oils, and diesel), alcoholic beverages, vehicles, soft drinks, mineral water, cigarettes and tobacco, luxury items, casino and games of chance (gambling, slot machines, lotteries, equestrian events and raffles). Tax rates are variable (percentage system) and for some items this tax is applied by charging a fixed amount per unit sold (specific system).

[411] *Customs Duties:* The Peruvian custom tariff structure includes three levels 0%, 6%, and 11%. There is a special regime that allows the temporary import o equipment without payment of customs duties, provided that the equipment i question will be re-exported within a period of eighteen months.

[412] *Financial Transactions Tax (ITF):* The ITF is levied on a series of financia transactions made through the Peruvian banking system, irrespective of the amount involved. In fact, this tax is applied to debits and credits in curren accounts, savings accounts, deposits, liquid asset funds, trust funds and other financial funds. The ITF paid is deductible for income tax purposes, as an expense o local resident companies and individuals.

[413] The 2020 rate for the ITF is 0.005%.

[414] *Immovable Property Transfer Tax (Alcabala):* Transfers of immovable property whether for consideration or not, are subject to a tax levied by municipalities. The acquirer will be the taxpayer. The rate of this tax is 3% of the transaction value. A non-leviable amount equivalent to UIT10 (USD13 030 approximately) is taken into account in order to determine the base.

[415] *Temporary Tax on Net Assets (ITAN):* This tax applies to taxpayers generating corporate income (third-category income) which is subject to the General Income Tax Regime (which also includes branches, agencies and other permanent establishments of non-resident corporations). Those who have not started operations, private education institutions, among others are exempted. ITAN is applied on the value of a company's net assets as at 31 December of the previous year. Certain assets may be deducted in order to determine the taxable base, including assets granted by concession, and shares, among others.

[416] The following rate will be applicable to the tax base in order to determine the tax due:

Years	*Rate*	*Net Assets*
2009 onwards	0.4%	Excess of PEN1 000 000 (approximately USD299 401)

[417] The tax paid may be credited against advance payments of income tax or the annual payment of income tax, or (in appropriate cases) a tax refund can be requested. This last procedure may apply in the case of tax losses or a minor tax assessed under the general regime rules, provided certain conditions are met.

[418] *Real Estate Property Tax:* The real estate property tax is an annual local tax imposed by the municipalities on the total value of rural or urban immovable property owned by an individual or a corporation within a local jurisdiction. The tax is applied at progressive rates as follows:

Taxable Base	*Rate*
Up to UIT15 (USD19 545)	0.2%
Between UIT15 and UIT60 (USD19 545 and USD78 181)	0.6%
More than UIT60 (USD78 181)	1.0%

[419] Concession holders of public works or services granted by the government are subject to this tax with respect to the property assigned to the contract or project during its term.

[420] *Employers' Contributions: Social Security (EsSalud):* Employers are obliged to register their employees in the national health system and must pay the equivalent of 9% from the monthly remuneration of each employee for this purpose. It is possible for employees to be affiliated to a Private Health Company (EPS) that is complementary to the service provided by EsSalud. In such cases, the employer must pay the cost of the service to the EPS and should pay 6.75% of the monthly salary to EsSalud.

[421] There are some benefits relating to the advanced recovery of the VAT Credit, and facilities for the payment of customs duties which are available to those companies involved in exploration, development and/or exploitation of natural resources. For example, the VAT Anticipated Recovery Regime grants the right to recover the VAT paid on the import and/or local acquisition of goods or services in the pre-production stage of a project, which will subsequently be used in the execution of such project, provided certain conditions are met.

[422] Also specific tax measures are in force in order to promote private investments in certain economic activities, such as mining, oil and gas, agriculture and generation of electricity by means of hydropower and other renewable resources. Some of these are measures which include benefits in connection with the acquisition of assets or goods necessary for the business.

14. TAX CONSOLIDATION GROUP RELIEF OF GAINS AND LOSSES

[423] Domiciled corporations may carry forward their Peruvian source net losses in order to set them off against future profits by using one of the following systems:

(i) Losses can be carried forward to set off against profits obtained in the immediately following next four fiscal periods counted from the year when the loss was generated. Under this regime, if a portion of the losses generated has not been offset within the four-year term, the taxpayer will lose the right to keep carrying forward the residual loss.

(ii) Losses obtained can be carried forward to set off against 50% of future profits. Under this system losses may be carried forward for an indefinite period.

[424] Exceptionally, net losses incurred in fiscal year 2020 may be carried forward to set off against profits obtained in the immediately following next five fiscal periods counted from the fiscal year 2021.

[425] For tax purposes, the consolidation of gains or losses within the 'business group' is not allowed. Each taxpayer, independently, must assess its own taxes.

[426] Under the scope of a reorganization of companies, the acquirer cannot carry forward the tax losses of the transferor. If the acquirer had tax losses at the time of the reorganization, it will only be allowed to offset against its own income an amount of tax losses no higher than the amount of its assets prior to the reorganization, and taking no account of any voluntary reappraisal.

[427] On the other hand, as of 1 January 2013 Controlled Foreign Corporation (CFC) rules came into force in order to avoid the deferral of Peruvian income tax liabilities derived from passive income (i.e., interest, royalties, capital gains, among others) received by foreign entities which are controlled by domiciled taxpayers. CFC rules apply, under certain conditions, to domiciled taxpayers who own a relevant participation in the capital of a foreign entity. As a consequence, the passive income obtained by the latter would be directly allocated to the domiciled taxpayer. Therefore, the owner will pay the income tax on foreign passive income obtained by these entities in the fiscal year when the income is actually received by them, and not at the time when a future dividend distribution is made by the foreign entity.

15. TAX CONSIDERATIONS ARISING ON M&A TRANSACTIONS

15.1. Mergers Corporate Income Tax

[428] Peruvian Income Tax Law, hereinafter referred to as 'the Law', has a special chapter dealing with the reorganization of companies. This includes the regime for mergers, spin-offs or any other kind of reorganization of companies as defined in the General Companies' Law, but excludes the transformation of companies.

[429] The Law has established three regimes for the reorganization of companies:

(1) If companies agree voluntarily to revalue their assets, the difference between the agreed higher value and the current net book value will be subject to the levy of income tax. In this case, the transferred goods and those of the acquirer will adopt the reappraised value as their current net book value. In this case, if as a result of the reorganization the companies are extinguished, they will have to pay the income tax generated by the

revaluation of the assets within the next three months following the reorganization. For depreciation purposes the value of the assets transferred pursuant to a reorganization will be the reappraised value minus the accumulated depreciation, and they will be considered as new assets for the assessment of the relevant lifetime.

The income tax determined as a result of the voluntary revaluation of assets cannot be offset against tax losses of the companies participating in the reorganization.

(2) If companies agree voluntarily to revalue their assets, the difference between the agreed higher value and the current net book value will not be levied with income tax to the extent that the higher value thus obtained is not distributed. In this case, the higher value given to the assets due to their voluntary reappraisal will have no effect for tax purposes and will not be deemed to affect their net book value in the relevant depreciation period. If the gain is distributed in cash or in kind by the company, it will be treated as taxable income of that company.

In this case, if the profit is distributed in cash or in kind by the company, it will be considered as taxable income of the company.

In addition, it is presumed (without the possibility of adducing any proof to rebut the said presumption) that the profits are distributed in any of the following cases:

(a) When the capital is reduced within the next four fiscal years from the fiscal year in which the reorganization took place, unless it is a compulsory capital reduction due to losses or is carried out pursuant to the General Companies' Law in order to re-establish the equilibrium between the capital and the net worth of the company as reduced due to losses.

(b) When a distribution of dividends is carried out, including the distribution of any revaluation surplus, inflation adjustments, grants and/or free distributable reserves, within the next four fiscal years from the fiscal year in which the reorganization took place.

(c) When a company carries out a spin-off and the shares or participations issued to its partners or shareholders as a result of the spin-off are transferred or cancelled by a subsequent reorganization, provided that:
   (i) the shares or participations transferred or cancelled represent more than 50% of the capital or voting rights of the total amount of shares or participations issued to the partners or shareholders of the spin-off company as a result of the reorganization; and
   (ii) the transfer or cancellation of the shares or participations is carried out prior to the end of the following fiscal year in which the spin-off was effective. In case the transfer or cancellation of shares took place at different times, it is presumed that the distribution was carried out when the transfer or cancellation exceeded the percentage referred to above.

(d) In this case, it is considered that the profit is distributed by the company acquiring the equity block, and therefore as taxable income of that company. This rule will be applied, disregarding any tax applicable on the capital gain obtained by the partners or shareholders for the transfer of their shares if it is the case.

(e) The taxable income referred to in the paragraphs above will be treated as obtained in the fiscal year in which the distribution was carried out. The payment of the tax under these provisions does not allow the companies to consider as a cost of the assets the highest value assigned due to the revaluation.

(3) If the companies do not agree voluntarily to revalue their assets, the transferred goods will have for the acquirer the same net book value that they used to have for the transferor, this also being the value applicable for depreciation purposes. In this case, the following presumptions are applicable, without the possibility of filing any proof to rebut the presumptions:

(a) The company acquiring one or more equity blocks split off from the other company, generates taxable income in respect of the difference between the fair market value (FMV) and the net book value of the assets received as a consequence of the reorganization, if the partners who received the shares or participations issued by the acquirer transfer, redeem or cancel such shares or participations, provided that:

(i) the shares or participations transferred, redeemed or cancelled represent more than 50% of the capital or voting rights of the total number of shares issued to the shareholders or partners of the spun-off company as a consequence of the reorganization; and

(ii) the transfer, redemption or cancellation of shares or participations has taken place prior to the end of the following fiscal year in which the spin-off is effective. If the transfer, redemption or cancellation of shares is performed at different times, it is presumed that the taxable income was generated at the moment when the transfer, redemption or cancellation exceeding the said percentage took place.

It is important to mention that the shareholders are jointly responsible for the income tax of the acquiring company. In addition, the shareholders must pay the income tax on the capital gain obtained on the transfer or redemption of the company's shares, if applicable.

(b) A company that segregates one or more equity blocks in a simple reorganization and redeems the shares or participations received as a consequence of the said reorganization generates taxable income on the difference between the FMV of the assets transferred as a consequence of the reorganization or the amount received from the company whose shares or participations are redeemed (whichever is the higher value) and the cost of the assets transferred, provided that:

(i) the shares or participations redeemed represent more than 50% of the capital or voting rights of the total shares or participations issued to the company as a consequence of the reorganization; and

(ii) the redemption of shares or participations takes place prior to the end of the fiscal year following that in which the reorganization is effective. If the redemption of shares or participations is carried out at different times, it is presumed that the taxable income was generated at the time when the redemption exceeding the relevant percentage referred to above took place.

[430] In the reorganization of companies, the acquirer is subject to the following rules:

- The acquirer cannot carry forward the tax losses of the transferor. If the acquirer had tax losses at the time of the reorganization, it will only be allowed to offset against its own income an amount of tax losses no higher than the amount of its assets prior to the reorganization, and taking no account of any voluntary reappraisal.
- The acquirer maintains the transferor's right to deduct as an expense the pre-operating expenses and the price of any intangibles with a short lifetime for their remaining term if the transferor chose to amortize them within ten years.
- The acquirer maintains the tax rights (tax credits, tax deductions and tax reimbursements) in proportion to the value of the assets received from the transferor as well as the tax liabilities of the transferor.

[431] Also, the Law establishes that for the assignment of rights due to a reorganization of companies, the acquirer needs to be subject to the same conditions and requirements to which the transferor was subject, in order to enjoy those rights.

[432] For the specific case of mergers, the benefits granted by a Tax Stability Agreement to any of the parties involved in the merger cannot be assigned to the other party unless prior authorization is obtained from the tax authority and from the competent administrative authority.

[433] These rules contained in the Law are applicable to the reorganization of Peruvian domiciled companies and, exceptionally, to the merger of branches of non-domiciled companies only if this is carried out as a consequence of the prior merger of their respective headquarters. Also, these rules are applicable to the reorganization of State-owned companies which are to be privatized.

[434] In the case of reorganization of companies, there is an express provision in the VAT Law exempting from the payment of VAT the transfer of goods carried out pursuant to the reorganization of companies.

[435] If the reorganization of companies involves the transfer of real estate, the acquirer will be levied with the Alcabala Tax, as defined in paragraph **[414]** above.

15.2. Purchase of Shares

[436] Where Peruvian companies are acquired by purchase of their shares, the capital gains derived from that transaction are subject to the levy of income tax.

Non-resident sellers must request from the SUNAT the issue of a certificate of the acquisition cost of the shares to be transferred in order to be taxed on net income. Otherwise, the transaction will be taxed on gross income. There are some conditions to take into consideration in order to obtain such certification.

[437] As mentioned above, VAT is charged at a rate of 18%, on (among other transactions) the sale of movables inside Peru. But, as shares are not regarded as movables by the VAT Law, their sale is not levied with that tax.

[438] The payment for the purchase of shares must be channelled through the Peruvian Bank System. Otherwise, the acquisition cost of the shares will not be deductible by the acquirer in any future sale of those shares.

15.3. Purchase of Assets

[439] The purchase of assets as a way of acquiring a business undertaking has no special treatment for income tax purposes. However, if the purchased assets are subject to depreciation, it will be possible for the Peruvian acquirer to continue to deduct depreciation as an expense for income tax purposes for the remaining lifetimes of the relevant assets.

[440] As mentioned above, VAT charges at a rate of 18%, among other transactions, the sale of movables inside Peru as well as the first sale of real estate carried out by constructors. If the assets of the company to be purchased are movables, that purchase will be levied with VAT. If the assets of the company to be purchased are real estate, that purchase will be levied with VAT only if it is the first sale of that real estate and if the transferor carried out its construction.

[441] The VAT paid by the acquirer for the purchase of those assets is a tax credit that can be deducted from VAT charged on the acquirer's sales in assessing the monthly amount of VAT to pay.

[442] The payment for the purchase of assets must be channelled through the Peruvian Bank System. Otherwise, the acquisition cost of the assets and their corresponding depreciation will not be deductible by the acquirer in any future sale of those assets.

[443] The transfer of real estate will also be levied with the Alcabala Tax, as defined in paragraph **[415]** above.

[444] Under the scope of a corporate reorganization, please see the tax rules mentioned in paragraph **[430]** above in connection with the valuation of assets.

[445] Under general market value rules, the SUNAT may adjust the price agreed by the parties so that it reflects the FMV. There are certain provisions established in the Income Tax Law with regard to the market value of assets, stock, securities, and services applicable to transactions between non-related entities. If the transaction is made between related entities, the market value will have to be assessed in accordance with transfer pricing rules. Note that Peruvian Income Tax Law established special rules that apply with respect to the acceptable cost in the following cases: (i) disposal of shares acquired for no consideration, where the shares are disposed of on or after 1 January 2013; (ii) disposal of shares acquired through capitalization of profits; and (iiii) disposal of intangible assets.

15.4. Acquisition Expenses

[446] Expenses incurred during the fiscal year by Peruvian domiciled corporations are generally deductible, provided that they are deemed necessary for obtaining third-category income as well as for maintaining the income source, unless expressly prohibited by law (e.g., personal expenses, income taxes, fines, donations not complying with certain conditions, certain provisions or reserves, VAT and excise tax, transfer of property without consideration, expenses supported by invoices that do not fulfil the requirements established by the Invoices Regulations, among others).[1] The assets acquired by Peruvian domiciled companies generate a cost which can be depreciated (the depreciation is deductible for income tax purposes).

[447] As a requirement for the deduction of costs and/or expenses, all services between related parties must meet the 'Benefit Test for Services'. Furthermore, taxpayers are required to keep and provide supporting documentation and information related to such services.

[448] The Benefit Test for Services is met whenever the service provides commercial or economic value to the service recipient, enhancing or maintaining its commercial position. The latter is in turn determined by evaluating whether an independent entity would have performed the service by itself or through a third party.

[449] As mentioned before, taxpayers are required to provide supporting documentation and information related to the services, in particular supporting the actual provision of the services; the nature of the services; the necessity for acquiring the services; as well as the costs and expenses incurred by the service provider and the allocation criteria used.

[450] In the case of low value-adding services, the costs and/or expenses of such services for tax purposes are assessed by adding all costs and expenses incurred by the service provider and the applicable markup, which may not be higher than 5% of the amount of costs and expenses incurred by the service provider.

[451] Low value-adding services have the following characteristics:

(i) they are of a supportive nature;
(ii) they are not part of the core business of the taxpayer or the multinational group, as applicable;

[1] As from 1 Jan. 2019, expenses incurred with non-resident entities will be deemed deductible in the fiscal year in which they are paid or credited within the legal term to file the annual income tax return.

(iii) they do not require the use of unique and valuable intangibles and do not lead to the creation of unique and valuable intangible; and
(iv) they do not involve the assumption or control of a high or significant risk and do not give rise to a significant risk for the service provider.

16. STRUCTURING THE INVESTMENT: WITHHOLDING TAXES

16.1. Withholding Taxes Applicable to Non-resident Individuals

[452] The following effective rates are applicable to non-domiciled individuals:

Concept	*Rate(%)*
Independent work	24
Dividends	5
Dependent work	30
Transfer of immovable property	30
Interests (when the payer is a domiciled corporation or individual that generates third-category income)	4.99
Interests (when the payer is a related party or the transaction is performed from or through tax havens[1])	30
Capital gains from the transfer of shares carried out within Peru (within Peruvian stock exchange)	5
Capital gains from the transfer of shares carried out abroad (out of the Peruvian stock exchange)	30
Royalties	30
Incomes of artists for shows performed within the country	15
Others	30

1. As from 1 January 2019, non-cooperating countries and subjects who earn income under a preferential tax regime will be included.

[453] Withholding taxes applicable to non-resident corporations.

[454] As a general rule, Peruvian source income obtained by non-resident entities is subject to a withholding tax rate of 30%. Nevertheless, the following special rates are applicable:

Dividends: A 5% withholding tax will be applicable on dividends.

Royalties: A 30% withholding tax rate is applicable on royalties. For this purpose, the Income Tax Law has defined royalties as the payment in consideration of use, or the privilege of using, brands, designs, or models; plans, secret processes, or formulas; author rights on literary, artistic, or scientific work; as well as any payment for the assignment of software or any information related to industrial, commercial or scientific experience.

Interest: Interest from credit operations will be subject to a withholding tax rate of 4.99%, provided:

- foreign currency must be paid in through the Peruvian Financial System;
- the purpose of the foreign loan must be related to the corporate business;
- the foreign creditor and the domiciled debtor are not related parties;
- credit must not accrue an annual interest of or exceeding LIBOR-plus 7 (USA, Canada, Europe) rates. If this condition is not fulfilled, only the surplus of the said rate will be subject to a 30% tax rate.

[455] Otherwise, a withholding tax rate of 30% will apply.

[456] Interest from bonds or debentures and other debts, financial instruments and deposits, according to the Financial System General Law, are subject to a withholding tax rate of 4.99%.

[457] Interest payable to non-domiciled corporations by domiciled banks and financial companies as a result of the usage in Peru of their credit lines abroad is subject to a withholding tax rate of 4.99%.

[458] *Lease of ships and aircraft:* Income derived from the lease of ships and aircraft is subject to a withholding tax rate of 10%.

[459] *Technical assistance:* Income derived from services that qualify as technical assistance will be levied with a withholding tax rate of 15% provided certain requirements are complied with.

[460] In this respect, the resident party must file with the SUNAT a report issued by an auditing firm certifying that the technical assistance has been effectively rendered. This requirement is needed if the income derived from services represents more than UIT140 (USD165 568 approximately).

[461] *Transfer of shares:* A withholding tax rate of 5% is applicable on the transfer of shares within the country, provided they are registered in the Stock Market Public Registry and negotiated within the Peruvian stock exchange. Otherwise, the transfer of shares will be deemed carried out abroad, in which case a withholding tax rate of 30% is applicable.

[462] This includes an indirect transfer of shares, which occurs when a non-resident company (either directly or indirectly through other companies) transfers shares of a resident company, provided that: (i) within the twelve months prior to the transfer, the FMV of the shares of the resident company, owned by the non-resident company, is equal to 50% or more of the FMV of the total shares of the non-resident company ('50% test') and the shares transferred represent 10% or more of the equity capital of the non-resident company ('the minimum rule'); or (ii) the non-resident company is domiciled in a tax haven, except when the taxpayer is able to prove that the condition described in (i) did not occur.[2]:

[463] On the other hand, please *see* paragraph **[399]** with regard to the Agreements to Avoid the Double Taxation entered into by Peru. Such agreements establish, among other provisions, maximum withholding tax rates in connection with passive income (i.e., dividends, interests and royalties).

16.2. Debt Financing and Thin Capitalization Rules

[464] Loans granted by non-resident entities to Peruvian subsidiaries or branches will be subject to the following rules.

[465] *Withholding Income Tax:* It will be the applicable withholding income tax rate of (30%) on the interest paid by the Peruvian subsidiary or branch.

[466] *Deduction of Interest (thin capitalization rules):* Interest accrued is deductible as an expense for income tax purposes. Such deduction will be subject to thin capitalization rules.

[467] In this context, interest originating in the indebtedness between related parties will only be deductible to the extent that such debt does not exceed three times the net worth of the Peruvian subsidiary ('thin capitalization rule').[3] Also, interest will only be deductible as an expense if the loans are related to the generation or production of income levied in Peru or to maintain the income producing source.

[2] As from 1 Jan. 2019 FMV has been included to the rules applicable to indirect transfer of shares:

- In order to verify the compliance of the 'minimum rule', both the transfer of shares made by the seller as well as those made by its related parties shall be considered.
- It has been included as a case of indirect transfer of shares when the total amount of the shares of the Peruvian entity (which are being indirectly transferred during any twelve-month period) is equal or higher than UIT40 000 (approximately, USD52 121 212).
- If no IT withholding is applicable, and the foreign transferor has a branch or other permanent establishment in Peru, the latter would be considered as joint and severally liable for the payment of the income tax arising from the indirect transfer. Moreover, such branch or permanent establishment would be obliged to provide information to Peruvian Tax Authorities regarding the transferred shares (such as FMV, participation percentages, capital increase or reduction, etc.)

[3] As from 1 Jan. 2019 to 12 Dec. 2020, such thin capitalization rule will apply to interest with respect to any loan, and not only to those granted between related parties, with some exemptions (e.g., financial system and insurance companies, taxpayers which annual revenue does not exceed approximately USD3 121 212). As from 1 Jan. 2021, new thin capitalization rules will apply. According to these, interest that exceeds 30% of the Earnings Before Interest, Taxes, Depreciation and Amortization (EBITDA) corresponding to the preceding fiscal year will not be deductible. Non-deductible interest may be carried forward considering certain limits.

16.3. Transfer Pricing Rules

[468] Special transfer pricing rules inspired by OECD guidelines are applicable in the case of transactions between related parties or executed towards, or from, tax haven countries, where prices assigned by the related parties affect the taxable interest (e.g., cause a lesser tax to be paid in Peru).

[469] Accordingly, under Peruvian transfer pricing legislation, the following methods can be used in order to determine the market price: (i) the compared uncontrolled price method (CUP), (ii) resale price method, (iii) cost plus method, (iv) profit split method, (v) residual profit split method, or (vi) the transactional net margin method; whichever is considered the most appropriate to reflect the arm's-length value.

[470] Moreover, taxpayers must comply with the following formal obligations:

- To keep detailed documentation and information about each transaction, when applicable, that supports the calculation of the transfer prices and the methodology used (among others) duly translated into Spanish, within the corresponding statute of limitations period of the tax obligation.
- Annually to file an affidavit with certain information, which will vary depending on the amount of annual income accrued by the taxpayer during a fiscal year and on whether it belongs to a local or a multinational group of companies, as follows:

Type of Affidavit	*Taxpayer*	*Annual Income Accrued*	*Information Reported*
Local Report[1]	All taxpayers	Taxpayer's annual income accrued > UIT2 300 (USD2 996 96)	Among other information: organizational structure; description of the inter-company transactions; benefit test for services; transfer pricing method used; financial statements corresponding to the related tax period.
Master File[2]	Taxpayers belonging to a local group[3]	Local group's annual income accrued > UIT20 000 (PEN26 060 606)	Among other information: organizational structure; a description of the business or businesses developed; a description of the transfer pricing policies regarding intangible assets and group financing; finance and fiscal status.

Type of Affidavit	*Taxpayer*	*Annual Income Accrued*	*Information Reported*
Country by Country Report[4]	Taxpayers qualified as headquarters of a multinational group[5, 6]	Multinational group's annual income accrued > PEN2 700 000 000 (USD351 818 181 818)	Among other information: global distribution of the income; losses; taxes paid; business activities regarding each of the entities belonging to the multinational group.

1. This new formal obligation has been in force since the 2017 fiscal year.

2. This new formal obligation has been in force since the 2018 fiscal year.

3. For this purpose, the term 'Group' has been defined as the group of persons, companies or entities related by way of property or control, obliged to formulate consolidated financial statements in accordance with the generally accepted accounting principles, or that would be obliged to do it if the shares issued by them were negotiated through a centralized negotiation mechanism.

4. This new formal obligation has been in force since the 2018 fiscal year.

5. For this purpose, the term 'Multinational Group' has been defined as a group composed of one or more persons, companies or entities with residence in Peru and one or more persons, companies or entities with foreign residence; or a group composed by one or more persons, companies or entities with tax residence in a jurisdiction taxed in a different jurisdiction on the activities carried out through a permanent establishment.

6. Taxpayers belonging to a multinational group, not qualified as the headquarters of the group, may also be obliged to submit the Country by Country Report if certain conditions are met. For instance, they are obliged to submit the Country by Country Report when the multinational group's annual income accrued is equal to or higher than PEN2 700 000 000 and the foreign headquarters of the group is not obliged to submit a Country by Country Report in their residence jurisdiction.

17. EMPLOYMENT CONSIDERATIONS

17.1. Legislative Framework

[471] There is no specific labour regulation related to corporate acquisitions and mergers. However, one of the Peruvian Labour Principles is the Continuity Principle.

[472] Under this principle, employees are transferred with the same benefits as they had in their former company before the corporate acquisition or merger was agreed, such as vacations, bonuses and severance payments. For such a transfer to occur, an agreement is required involving the participation of the merging company, the merged company and the employee. This agreement should be filed with the Peruvian Labour Authority and should include a list of all the labour benefits the employee already has in order to avoid any future labour dispute. If the employee refuses to be transferred to the new company, the merging company has the option to dismiss him.

[473] An alternative possibility could be that the merging company hires the employee under a new labour agreement. In this context, the merging company and the employee must agree on the terms of the new labour agreement. This alternative involves as a first step that the employee must terminate his labour agreement with the merged company which must pay the employee all his labour benefits.

[474] The labour regime is ruled by different laws, especially by Supreme Decree No. 003-97-TR, which regulates the rights and obligations of the employee, the reasons and circumstances of any employee dismissal, including the cases of collective termination contracts, and the main hiring regimes.

[475] Additionally the labour regime is governed by:

- Legislative Decree No. 713, which regulates the entitlement to thirty calendar days' vacation and the payment of the vacation period.
- Supreme Decree No. 001-97-TR, which regulates the Compensation for Time Served (CTS), which is given to private sector employees who work a minimum of four hours per day.
- Law No. 27735, which regulates legal bonuses (one for Independence Day and one for Christmas) which employees are entitled to receive.
- Law No. 29783, Health and Safety Law in the Workplace, which regulates minimum standards to prevent occupational risks.

[476] It is important to note that, according to Peruvian Legislation there are no mandatory or minimum clauses for a labour agreement. Thus, the parties could freely regulate their obligations and introduce additional and higher benefits than those legally established.

[477] However, it is usual to include the following clauses: (i) the parties' obligations, (ii) the object of the labour agreement, (iii) the duties of the employee, (iv) the term of the agreement, (v) the salary, (vi) the labour benefits, (vii) the trial period, (viii) confidentiality terms, (ix) jurisdiction, (x) applicable law, (xi) personal data protection of the employee, among others.

17.2. Employment Protection

[478] According to Peruvian Legislation, there is only one employment protection, which relates to arbitrary dismissal. The employer can only dismiss for fair reasons.

[479] Fair reasons for dismissal include: (i) serious offences; (ii) criminal conviction for fraud; and (iii) disability of the employee.

[480] The following are considered as serious offences:

(i) Non-compliance with working obligations.

(ii) Deliberate and repeated decrease in performance in the undertaking of the employee's tasks or their volume or quality.
(iii) Actual or attempted appropriation of property or services of the employer.
(iv) Use or delivery to third parties of confidential information of the employer.
(v) Unauthorized removal of property.
(vi) Repeated attendance under the influence of alcohol, drugs or narcotics.
(vii) Acts of violence, serious lack of discipline, perjury or verbal or written statements made to the detriment of the employer.
(viii) Intentional damage to facilities, works, equipment and other property belonging to or in the possession of the company.
(ix) Unjustified absence from work for more than 3 consecutive days, 5 days within a period of 30 days or 15 days during a period of 180 calendar days.
(x) Failure to fulfil work obligations involving breach of the obligation of good faith.
(xi) Repeated non-performance of orders related to the work.
(xii) Repeated untimely paralysis of work verified by the Administrative Labour Authority.
(xiii) Non-observance of the internal working regulations or the regulation of safety and industrial hygiene.

[481] Consequently, an employee who is unfairly dismissed has the right to receive a special indemnity and/or a severance payment or to claim reinstatement in the job.

[482] If the employee is hired under a fixed term agreement, the special indemnity and/or severance payment is equivalent to 1.5 monthly salary payments for each month remaining until the end of the agreement, with a maximum of twelve monthly salary payments. Periods of time less than one year will be paid proportionally.

[483] An employee under a non-fixed term agreement has as special indemnity an amount equivalent to 1.5 monthly salary payments per year of service with a maximum of twelve monthly salary payments. Periods of time less than one year will be paid proportionately. In the case of business transfers, there is no specific employment or labour regulation governing the implications of and circumstances arising in such cases. However, there is a principle of continuity based on the protection from arbitrary dismissal. Thus, when all the assets are transferred to a new company that includes the transfer of goods this does not imply the transfer of the employees. The buyer of the business, the seller and the employees must agree to the transfer of the employees. Of course, if the seller of the business sells the business and does not terminate the labour contract in accordance with the law and does not pay the social benefits to the employee, the employees in question will probably try to obtain a judicial measure ordering the buyer to hire them to continue working in the operation. In this case, to avoid any future problem, the employees must receive an offer to continue working with the buyer of the business. According to Peruvian Legislation, employees are not entitled to management representation. The company board is the one which decides the administration of the company.

In the case of a transfer of shares, the employees cannot block the transfer of shares.

[484] The transfer of a business is not regulated. The employer is not obliged to consult with the employees on the sale of a business. However, as the seller probably wants to transfer the employees to the buyer, then the seller, the buyer and the employees should sign an agreement. If as a result of the transfer of the unit the employees lose their work, the employees could obtain a precautionary order to stop the transfer of the asset because their right to the job is not guaranteed.

[485] The rights of works councils are stated by law. Supreme Decree No. 010-2003-TR, which regulates collective labour relations, states that works councils represent the employees and they only have negotiation rights. Consequently, they do not have strong rights as unions.

[486] Mass redundancies and/or mass layoffs are regulated by law, only under specific circumstances, and must follow a procedure at the Administrative Labour Authority. Otherwise, an employee who is unfairly dismissed has the right to receive a special indemnity and/or severance payment. To start the process of collective termination, the employer would have to reduce his workforce by more than 10%. If the percentage is less than 10%, then the collective termination is not possible.

[487] The protection against arbitrary dismissal is recognized in the Peruvian Constitution. However, this protection applies only after the trial/probation period has expired.

[488] Peruvian legislation defines the first three months of the engagement as the trial and/or probation period, but this could be extended to six months or one year if the employee is regarded as a manager or as trusted personnel, or if he has to be trained. A 'manager' is understood as an employee who represents the employer before third parties and/or who has managerial and control functions. Trusted personnel are employees who work directly with management personnel.

[489] Therefore, employees cannot simply be dismissed at any time or in any circumstances. For the dismissal to be valid, it must be for the reasons and in the circumstances stated by law (e.g., for the fair reasons for dismissal referred to above).

[490] Consequently, an employee who is unfairly dismissed has the right to receive a special indemnity and/or a severance payment or to claim reinstatement in the job.

[491] To dismiss an employee, the employer must follow a special process established by the law.

[492] When an employer wishes to terminate a labour contract, it is common for the employer to negotiate for the employee to resign in order to avoid the risk of reinstatement.

[493] Labour law does not distinguish between white collar workers and blue collar workers. Their rights are the same and any differences are minimal (e.g., blue collar workers receive their salary on a daily basis whereas white collar workers usually receive their salary on a monthly basis).

18. LABOUR COSTS AND WORKING CONDITIONS

[494]

(i) *Minimum Wage*: The remuneration is determined by the employer and the employee according to their respective interests and/or abilities. The tax law has established some tax limitations in cases where the employee is a shareholder.

Nevertheless, Peruvian law establishes a minimum wage which the employer is obliged to observe no matter what type of activity is undertaken by the employee.

Currently, the minimum remuneration is fixed at PEN930.00 (Approximately USD259.77). There are minimum wages for different kinds of activity.

(ii) *Compensation for Time Served (CTS)*: CTS is given to private sector employees who work a minimum of four hours per day.

Biannually (May and November), as much as one-twelfth of the applicable remuneration earned by individual employees in the months of April and October will be deposited by employers for the benefit of employees, according to the number of full months worked. Fractions of the month must be deposited proportionately.

Applicable remuneration is defined as the basic compensation plus any amounts earned by the employee in cash or in goods by way of consideration for their work, provided that they are actually made available to the employee.

Exclusions from applicable remuneration for this purpose include special bonuses, profit sharing, employment conditions cost, Christmas basket items and the like, the value of fares necessary for the worker's attendance at the workplace, annual birthday and similar types of distribution, any expenses met for employees by the employer, such as transport, business expenses, clothing allowances and any other expenses which are reasonably necessary for the purpose of the employment but which will not constitute a benefit or enhancement of the net worth of the worker.

The applicable remuneration will take into account: average overtime, commission, and bonuses. All deposits must be made at institutions within the Peruvian financial system.

(iii) *Annual Vacation*: For each full year of service, employees working a minimum of four hours per day and who have achieved their required quota in the year are entitled to thirty calendar days' vacation.

The payment for the vacation period will be equivalent to the remuneration the employee would receive for that period if he were working. In this calculation, the average commission will also be taken into account.

In the event that the employee does not take the vacation earned within a year, he will be entitled to: (i) remuneration for the work carried out; (ii) remuneration for the vacation earned and not taken; and (iii) indemnity remuneration equivalent to the remuneration for not having taken the vacation time.

(iv) *Legal Bonuses*: Employees have the right to receive two bonuses per year; one for Independence Day and one for Christmas. These must be paid on the 15th of July and December, respectively.

In order to have the right to receive such bonuses employees must be working for the company during the month when the bonus was paid, or be on vacation, or paid licence, or earning the corresponding subsidies. If employees have been working for less than six months, the bonus will be in proportion to the number of months worked.

The bonus is made up of the basic remuneration plus any other amounts which are fixed and permanently earned by the employee and which are at the employee's disposal.

(v) *Profit Sharing*: Employees of companies with more than twenty employees and earning incomes are entitled to share in their company's profits according to the percentages laid down by law, as per the following table:

Activity	*Percentage*
Fishing companies	10%
Industrial companies	10%
Telecommunication companies	10%
Wholesalers, retailers and restaurants	8%
Mining companies	8%
Other activities	5%

(vi) *Family Allowance*: Employees of private companies who do not have their remuneration regulated by collective bargaining, will receive, regardless of the date of commencement of employment, the equivalent of 10% of the Minimum Remuneration. This is provided to employees who have one or more dependents under the age of 18. Where the dependent is over 18 years old and on a higher education or university study course, this benefit will be extended until such studies are completed, up to a maximum of six years after reaching that coming of age.

(vii) *Life Insurance*: Employees are entitled to life insurance. The employer is obliged to contract the insurance policy from the beginning of the worker's employment and to pay the corresponding premiums.
If the worker dies or has an accident, causing permanent disability, and the employer has failed to comply with this obligation, the employer must pay his beneficiaries the value of the insurance established by law.

(viii) *National Health System (SNS)*: The health services for which the Peruvian Social Security Institute (EsSalud, today) is responsible was created by Decree-Law No. 22482.

Furthermore, the Law for the Modernization of Social Security, approved by Law No. 26790, includes private sector participation in the provision of medical services through Business Health Services (EPS).

[495] The law requires that employees transferred to an EPS must continue contributing to EsSalud and that the contribution must be paid by the employer.

[496] However, the EPS will only provide certain services – those which are the most common and at the same time less complex, while the most frequent and more complicated services will still be provided by EsSalud.

[497] *Collective bargaining agreements*. – In Peru, the unions only represent 5% of the workforce. Those unions generally are not powerful but can sometimes be problematic.

19. PENSIONS

[498] Pensions and/or superannuation provisions are legal contributions stated by law (*see* our comments above).

[499] The contribution is paid by the employee and the employer must withhold the relevant percentage from the employee's remuneration.

[500] According to Peruvian Legislation, employees have the right to choose the system into which they will contribute: (i) the National Pension System under the responsibility of the Government Pension Fund Office – ONP (the monthly contribution is 13%); or, (ii) a Private Pension System managed by Pension Fund Management Companies – AFP (the monthly contribution depends on the AFP selected, approximately 12.9% of the monthly remuneration). Consequently, it is only the employees themselves who can change their pensions system and/or their contributions. The pension contribution is paid by the employee and the employer must withhold the percentage from the employee's remuneration.

20. RETENTION OF KEY MANAGEMENT AND EMPLOYEES

[501] The only effective way of ensuring the continuation of individual employees is the monthly remuneration or an attractive compensation package from the employer. Employees have the right to end the labour relationship at any time on thirty days prior notice to the employer.

[502] There are no statutory provisions regulating the application of non-compete clauses. However, the Peruvian Constitution guarantees the right to work. In view of this constitutional guarantee, a non-compete clause could be regarded as a restriction of the liberty to exercise a profession or an activity. Thus this type of agreement could be considered illegal and null by the courts.

[503] In labour agreements or in certain termination agreements, it is very common to introduce a provision for non-competition by the employee after the labour agreement is finished. Nevertheless, this kind of clause could also conflict with the right to work established by the Constitution.

[504] For this reason employers sometimes agree to pay to their employees or former employees a reasonable amount of money for non-competition, and under these arrangements the employee or former employees agree not to carry out or develop certain defined activities for a reasonable period of time.

21. TREATMENT OF FOREIGN EMPLOYEES

[505] Employers in Peru are able to hire foreign workers as long as they do not represent more than 20% of all the personnel, and their remuneration does not exceed 30% of all the payroll of salaries and wages.

[506] However, employers are able to disregard these limits and request exemption in the following cases:

- (i) specialized professional or technical personnel;
- (ii) management and/or general personnel in a new corporate activity, or in cases of corporate restructuring;
- (iii) teachers hired to provide advanced education or basic or secondary education in private foreign schools or in the teaching of languages in national private schools or specialized language centres;
- (iv) personnel belonging to companies in the public sector or private companies which are party to contracts with organizations, institutions or companies in the public sector; and
- (v) any other cases established by Supreme Decree, in line with specialization, qualification or experience criteria.

However, the following cases are not subject to any formalities or limitations on hiring foreigners:

(i) foreigners who have a Peruvian spouse, ascendants, descendants or brothers;
(ii) foreigners enjoying immigrant visas;
(iii) foreigners whose country of origin has reciprocal labour or dual citizenship agreements;
(iv) personnel of foreign companies engaged in the international ground, air or maritime transport service, with a foreign flag and registration;
(v) foreign personnel working for multinational service companies or banks subject to the legal provisions issued in respect of these specific cases;
(vi) foreigners who, by virtue of bilateral or multilateral agreements entered into with the Peruvian government, render their services in Peru;
(vii) foreign investors, whether or not they waive their rights to repatriate their capital or profits deriving from their investments, provided this is at least equivalent to 5 Tax Units during the term of the contract; and
(viii) artists, athletes and, generally, persons acting in public events within the country during a maximum period of three months of the year.

[507] Labour agreements for foreign personnel must be in writing and for fixed terms of up to three years, which could be successively renewable for similar periods.

[508] It should be noted that foreigners are unable to render service as employees (nor receive remuneration from the employer company) at any time in which the labour agreement and work visa proceedings are in force.

[509] To obtain this kind of visa it is first necessary to obtain approval from the Labour Ministry for a Labour Agreement with a Peruvian Company. The proceedings before the Labour Ministry can take at least five days or, in cases where it proves necessary to present new information, a maximum of three weeks.

[510] Once the Labour Agreement is approved, the change of migratory status can be initiated (tourist and/or business to work visa) with the Migratory Department. These proceedings can take approximately forty-five days.

[511] Once the work visa is granted, it is necessary to obtain a Foreign Card. After the grant of the Foreign Card, the employee can render his services to the local company.

[512] *Non-residents for tax purpose*: Income earned in Peru by a non-resident for tax purposes is subject to income tax at a rate of 30%.

[513] Residence for tax purposes is determined by the situation of the foreigner at the beginning of the fiscal year, and if the foreigner remains in Peru for more than 183 days in the prior fiscal year he will be regarded as resident for tax purposes.

[514] It is important to note that the labour relationship of foreign employees is regulated by the same legislative framework as for national employees. Consequently, foreign employees have the same rights and employers must comply with the same social benefits and legal contributions in their favour.

[515] Under Peruvian legislation, being a director is an onerous duty. The amount of the retribution is stated by the statute of the company. Otherwise, the annual shareholders' meeting must determine the amount. Foreigners can be appointed as directors.

22. ACCOUNTING TREATMENT

[516] According to Article 33 of the Peruvian Income Tax Regulations, accounting must be carried out based on the Generally Accepted Accounting Principles applicable in Peru.

[517] Also, bear in mind that Peru has approved the following international accounting rules as mandatory:

- IAS Numbers 1, 2, 7, 8, 10, 12, 16, 19, 20, 21, 23, 24, 26, 27, 28, 29, 32, 33, 34, 36, 37, 38, 39, 40 and 41.
- IFRS Numbers 1, 2, 3, 4, 5, 6, 7, 8, 9, 10, 11, 12, 13, 14, 15 16 and 17. Moreover, certain Standards Interpretations Committee (SIC) Numbers 7, 10, 25, 29 and 32 and International Financial Reporting Interpretations Committee (IFRIC) Numbers 1, 2, 5, 6, 7, 12, 14, 16, 17, 19, 20, 21, 22 and 23 rulings are applicable.
- The accounting books and records must be prepared in Spanish and in local Peruvian currency. If a taxpayer carries out a transaction in foreign currency, in order to register the transaction in the accounting records, the amount of the foreign currency must be converted to Peruvian currency using the exchange rate published by the Superintendence of Banking and Insurance in the Official Legal Gazette 'El Peruano'. Additionally, if a taxpayer receives or makes foreign investments in foreign currency he may be authorized to keep records in the foreign currency.

[518] Finally, Law No. 28951 establishes that the accounting information contained in the accounting books and records will require certification by a certified public accountant in order to be officially valid before third parties.

Made in the USA
Monee, IL
13 March 2026

46140462R00059